# Seminars for the
# Financial Advisor

## Build Your Business With Events and Create a Referral Generating Machine

## Adri Miller-Heckman
### President and Owner of Adri Miller Consulting

Femme Osage Publishing
St Louis, Missouri
2009

First Edition

ISBN: 978-1-934509-25-8

Library of Congress Control Number: 2009928665

Printed in the United States of America.

First printing: 2009

Cover illustration by:
    Cyanotype.ca

Published by:
    Femme Osage Publishing
    1301 Colby Drive
    Saint Peters, Missouri 63376
    FemmeOsagePublishing.com

## Dedication:

I dedicate this book to my husband Jim. Through his constant patience and undying support, I am living a life I once just dreamed about.

I would be remiss if I did not thank all my clients who have worked with me over the years providing the materials, the stories and the lessons in seminars that helped to create this book.

# Table of Contents

# Preface

## My Love Affair with Seminars.

Since I began my career in the 1980's, I have had a love affair with seminars. I do not know of any other method as effective in providing a valuable service to my clients, developing prospects and turning them into clients, while leveraging my time and growing my practice exponentially. Through the use of seminars, I built a very successful practice with clients I love, while working just 6 to 8 hours a day 5 days a week – while having fun at the same time.

I did not learn the magic of seminars from a book, nor did I take a course on how to create a seminar program. I learned through experience. My 22-years of managing clients, working with and training financial advisors, and experiencing the constant changes in the industry all added to my foundation of knowledge. Since writing the first version of this book, back in 2005, I can tell you that things have changed dramatically. The question is, are seminars, or as I prefer to call them, "Events," still a viable form of generating new business? The answer is yes, but I don't want to jump ahead of myself. Let's go back to where it all started.

I began applying my skills in the late 1980's. When I was a sales assistant, my branch hosted large events (about 300 people) twice a year. The lack of organization drove me crazy. I knew they could be so much more productive and effective. Even though I was a just sales assistant at the time, I volunteered to take on the responsibility for organizing these events. The advisors were now able to sit with their guests, dramatically increasing their opportunities to develop new relationships. Without this organization and system of planning, it was just a big event, costing a lot of time, energy and especially money, and rarely if ever paying off.

I learned I was good at it and enjoyed planning successful events. Later, as a branch administrator, I was asked to create a seminar program so the advisors in the branch would only have to invite their clients and show up at the event. This is when I began a monthly program featuring different professional money managers. In planning, organizing, and implementing these events, I gleaned what worked well and how to leverage a successful seminar program.

In 1995, I was a single mother left to raise three young children on my own. The meager salary of my support staff position was clearly not going to permit me to achieve even a fraction of the security and opportunities I wanted to provide my children. I made a decision that would allow me to use all of the knowledge I'd gained and change my life forever.

My branch manager asked me to join the sales force as a financial advisor (FA). This was the beginning of my future and my passion for training others. The opportunity to become a financial advisor with unlimited upside earning potential meant I could provide a great life for my children while still having the flexibility to enjoy time with them. I could not wait to start.

During my three months of training, it became evident that I was not going to be able to build my business through traditional methods. I did not have 10 hours a day or Saturdays to spend in the office. My children were, and continue to be, my highest priority, so my role as a financial advisor would have to revolve around my responsibilities as a mother.

After training, I met with my branch manager to discuss my plans for building my business. At the time, women made up a small percentage of the sales force. The methods for building a practice had yet to be modified to fit the demands of a working mother. Fortunately, my branch manager was well acquainted with my work ethic and family situation. His only mandate was that I get in front of five new prospects each week.

Although I was very good at cold calling, I knew I did not have the time available to make enough calls to set up five appointments a week. I had to come up with a method that allowed me to better leverage my time and energy on a consistent basis. Considering my experience, I quickly concluded that seminars were my method of choice.

I didn't know it yet, but I had started my business with a huge advantage. I already had a clearly defined target market and, although I did not think of it as my mission at the time, I knew what I was trying to achieve for my clients. This was probably the most important factor leading to my success. My target market was women over 50, living in Newport Beach, California. These women were either currently responsible for their own financial affairs or would be at some point in the near future. They typically lacked the knowledge and confidence to make good financial decisions, creating tremendous worry and uncertainty in their lives.

Because these women were a reflection of my own mother's situation, I had first hand knowledge of their issues and worries. By identifying their key concerns, I was able to develop a multi-tiered seminar program that addressed each of these points. I held women's workshops in my branch conference room. I hosted monthly luncheon events at a local five star restaurant, featuring different money managers, and incorporated four specialty women's events each year and even held an annual seminar. My understanding of my market, combined with my consistent event program, allowed me to build a successful practice, spend quality time with my children, and left enough time to reenergize myself and continue looking forward to my next event.

As I reflect back on my days as a rookie in the bullpen, the image I have is of a strong desire to succeed, combined with an exceptional work ethic. Let me explain what I mean by this.

At the time, I was the only female rookie in our branch, possibly even in the region. In the office, young men surrounded me, some married but most not, who had all the time in the world to focus on building their business.

I sprinted into the office by 6:30 each morning. I was busy from the moment I walked in until I sprinted out the door at 3:00, to pick up my kids from school.

I had a limited amount of time to spend on my practice and made every minute count. I did not have the luxury to become bogged down with issues that did not have an impact on growing my business. I had a clear focus to my days, which typically consisted of filling and marketing my events, following up with former event participants and generating production.

I saw many of my colleagues (other rookies) spending many more hours in the office yet generating dismal results. I learned from this experience. Your work has less to do with the amount of time you spend than how you spend your time. My seminar program encouraged me to stay focused on business building activities ONLY.

It was not until much later, when I became a Smith Barney National Training Officer, that I noticed I had defied the odds and built a great practice. Even though I had little time and no money, I'd found a way to succeed while many of my peers failed.

Since then, I have spent the past nine years coaching, training, and teaching other financial advisors the art of seminars. This book is a reflection of what I provide my clients on an individual basis. I designed this program so that you too can plan, create, and implement your own seminar program; a program planned around people you love to work with, while enjoying more time for family and greater passion for your business.

# Introduction
## Are You Ready For This?

Seminars are not new. For thousands of years, people have used group gatherings as a method of leveraging their ability to send a message, attract interest, build relationships or inspire change in others. Seminars continue to be an effective business tool to promote a concept, sell a product, or educate clients or customers. They are highly utilized in the financial services industry, however there has been little information, training, or guidance available on how to create an event that actually works and achieves the objective.

## You Don't Have to be a Natural

What prevents many FA's from hosting events is the fear of public speaking. The thought of getting up in front of a room full of participants can be overwhelming to even the best advisor. Have no fear; you will find as you read this book that the only skill you really need to host a good event is the ability to engage in conversation. Later in the book, you will learn how easy it is to create dialogue, generate further interest in what you do, enhance your image as a professional and motivate participants to become clients.

Granted, there are some people who are naturally gifted public speakers, able to inspire and engage the audience with little to no training. That is not the case for most people. Nevertheless, in today's environment, you have a choice. You can host events based on a conversational style, OR you can hire a coach or join a speaking group in order to hone your skills as a public speaker. Either way, you will benefit from the impact seminars can have on growing your business.

Usually when you give a seminar, the objective is to move the listener to action, open an account, schedule a meeting with you, or buy a particular product or service. Whether you are a natural speaker or want to develop your speaking skills, this program will help you increase your energy, enthusiasm, and passion for the business – characteristics that make your events generate optimum results.

If you are like many of us, you have sought out the hundreds of books written by experts who provide volumes of information, tips, and checklists and vast arrays of ideas and suggestions on types of seminars, styles of invitations, and presentation tips, hoping to find the "secret." All this information is great, if you are one of those informational junkies. However, too much information can be paralyzing. What you really want is the formula, the systematic process that you can implement today and build on tomorrow.

This book is designed to give you just that. It has been developed specifically to give you enough information to produce an effective seminar program, present a message that leads to action, and critically, follow up after the event – all focused on generating business. I have deliberately limited your options and choices to keep things simple. I focus on proven methods that work specifically for the financial advisor. I have included pages of sample invites, scripts, and checklists, all created by other advisors who have been successful in developing their own event program. This will become the foundation of all your events. Once you have mastered the process and developed your core skills, I encourage you to read those other books with seminar tips. They will provide great additional value. Until then, I highly recommend you stick to this program and focus on getting the systems and processes up and running first.

## Who Should Read This?

This book is written specifically for financial advisors:

- Who are looking for a new method to grow their practice, while becoming energized and excited about their business and the value they provide clients.
- Who recognize the value seminars can have on their practice, but cannot seem to find the right formula to make their seminars effective.
- Who realize that just as markets evolve, so too must events and seminars in order to continue generating results.
- Who want to create an easy opportunity for existing clients to provide referrals and introductions to new prospective clients.
- Who understand the value of using multiple prospecting/ marketing methods to grow their business.
- Who want to create more opportunities to get face to face with existing and prospective clients, while leveraging their time, energy and resources.
- Who are ready to grow their business in less time and with less effort.

This step-by-step, proven method works and is ready to put into place today. You will find worksheets to complete, lists to compile, and questions to answer. Each chapter prepares you for the next, which ties together to create a well-developed program that is simple to implement and adds value to your practice. To make it even easier, I provide you with tons of sample materials that will help you get started.

The next 13-chapters work through each step in the process. By the end, you will have a customized seminar program, driven by the needs of your target market, and a repeatable process that leverages your marketing strategies and saves you time and energy. You will have a calendar of events, driven by a theme, which works synergistically to accelerate the growth of your practice. We will look at presentation skills and address many methods specifically designed to engage the audience and motivate them to action. Finally, you will learn how to use the follow-up call as your final push toward achieving your goal.

When you complete this book, you will feel excited about your business with a new vision of your future and the potential for your practice. In addition, you will have rediscovered the passion for the business you once thought lost.

## Are You Ready to Commit?

You should be very familiar with this step in the sales process and understand how important it is to get a commitment before moving forward. My book is no different. To make this program work, you must be willing to commit time each week to develop the worksheets and implement the process. You must be willing to open your mind to new ideas and think creatively. Let go of any preconceived ideas about seminars.

To make this process truly valuable, I ask that you make the following commitments. Are you ready to...

- Double your referrals by implementing a program that becomes effortless?
- Increase your assets and accounts by designing your program around the core needs and concerns of your target market?
- Enhance client loyalty and increase product penetration by developing a streamlined marketing plan?
- Continue to stay focused and energized each month as you prepare and implement your next event?

If you answered "yes" to all of these questions, grab a pen, spiral notebook, and a highlighter and let's get started.

# Chapter 1

## Partnerships and Pork Bellies

What you will learn:
- The value of seminars in the past
- What clients are looking for
- How seminars can help you grow your business
- How to incorporate seminars with your marketing plan
- The many benefits of seminars today

The purpose of this chapter is to help you recognize the evolution of the financial services industry and the impact of those changes on building your business. We uncover how seminars have played a role in helping advisors build their business and the benefits of utilizing seminars today.

To understand my method and the value it will have on your practice, it is important to review the evolution of our industry and our role as financial advisors today vs. yesterday.

I started in the financial services industry in 1982. At the time, limited partnerships were the rage, and tax shelters were the haven for investors. Cold calling was the most effective method of growing your practice, and there were few or no compliance issues. Opening accounts and generating gross was all about your product. If you did not have a product to sell, you did not have a business. I remember cold calling on commodities, if you can believe that, selling pork bellies and soybeans over the phone. Amazingly, it worked.

In the 1990's, there was a shift toward fee-based business and the focus became financial planning. "Limited Partnership" became a dirty word, and mutual funds and collateralized mortgage obligations (CMO's) began filling the void. Although cold calling was still a viable form of prospecting, the focus changed from product to the need for financial plans. Instead of selling the features and benefits of a product or investment, we learned to profile and create the need for a full financial plan. With this more comprehensive approach, it became more important to develop a "relationship" with a prospect before they would typically become your client. One of the ways to accelerate this relationship was through seminars. Seminars created a more efficient method of getting in front of more people while enhancing relationships. Seminars began playing an effective role in generating volumes of potential clients. A product-focused breakfast seminar at Polly's Pies or Denny's was not uncommon. Volume, volume, volume – the more the merrier.

> **In the 1990's seminars created a more efficient method of getting in front of more people.**

Though the importance of financial planning and the value of fee based business continued to be the foundation to building relationships and marketing your practice, as we neared the end of the 90's, it became all about performance and fees. The technology boom created unreal expectations, increased the number of *Do It Yourselfers* and warranted the questioning of our fees. During this time, I became a national training officer for Smith Barney. Much of our effort was to help advisors defend and justify their fees.

Although the markets were booming, and assets under management were growing with little to no effort on the part of the advisors, this had to be one of the most challenging times not just to open new accounts, but to maintain existing relationships.

As with all things in life, change is inevitable. What goes up must come down proved to be more than true. As the first decade of the 21st century ends, we are experiencing one of the most unprecedented times any of us have ever seen. In what some consider a global recession, performance today is determined by who has lost the least amount of money. Investors are reeling from the ongoing volatility in the markets. Investors, especially those who have lost the majority of their retirement assets, are still processing the reality of these events.

As with any crisis, we experience a multitude of emotions, from denial, anger, bargaining, depression and finally acceptanc++e. Although everyone experiences these stages in their own unique order, I find that clients are beginning to move more into the acceptance stage, looking for solutions and recovery options. So, what is it that clients are looking for today? What is it that will compel an investor to change advisors? What would motivate a do-it-yourselfer to hire an advisor? SERVICE.

Today, 85% of clients are not happy. Is it the lack of performance causing their dissatisfaction, or lack of communication? Is it the lack of service and value, so needed during these volatile times and yet lacking? In today's environment, products do not open accounts. People don't come to us as new clients because of the importance of financial planning or the performance of our products.

The one overriding factor that can create the desire and interest to move accounts is the service and value you provide. Thus, seminars and events performed and provided on a regular basis can provide the opportunity for clients and prospects to get the communication, the education, the advice and the guidance they expect, plus that personal touch and attention they are so thirsting for.

> **The one overriding factor that can create the desire and interest to move accounts is the service and value you provide.**

Over time, the term "stockbroker" was replaced with "financial consultant." Now, the term is moving toward "wealth manager." What was a low-touch transactional business in the 80's, became a high-touch, fee-based business in the 90's. Where performance was the catalyst for change, service has become the foundation to growing and maintaining a healthy practice. Where we were content to sell just stocks and bonds, we now are looking to provide insurance, lending, banking, estate planning, and a multitude of products and services that extend our reach well beyond the stock and bond markets. Where we were content to present our performance as proof of our efforts, we are now looking to sell and market our service and the intrinsic value that comes with being our client.

As we continue moving more and more towards total wealth management, specialization is becoming critical to survival. Depth of resources is the foundation of today's practice. A high level of client service and added benefits build client loyalty and inspires referrals. Our relationships with our clients are reaching new levels, becoming stronger and more complex and crossing generations. All of this creates greater demands on our time and affords even less time to develop new business. This leads us to the new push for partnerships. Partnerships are becoming critical to building dynamic businesses that can continue to focus on organic growth while actively pursuing external growth.

At the same time, the do-not-call list has reduced the efficiency of cold calling; large volume seminars are filled with empty seats and lack the intimacy necessary for developing the trust so necessary today; increased competition has diluted our prospecting efforts. So, how do we find new clients and grow our business in this new environment, while balancing high levels of client service? Seminars.

> **Seminars allow you to find new clients and grow your business while increasing client service.**

Just as our role as financial advisors has become more dynamic, so must our marketing strategy. Each piece of our strategy must work in conjunction with the others, and address a multitude of issues in a variety of methods that allow us to penetrate a selected target market. This seminar program will be the thread that weaves all of your marketing efforts together. It will emphasize your value as a financial advisor. Your strategy will become the foundation of the service you provide your clients. It will also differentiate you from all other financial advisors who continue to build their business the old-fashioned way.

> **An effective seminar program is the thread that weaves all your marketing efforts together.**

Although there is a time and place for large-volume seminars, the bulk of our program will be smaller, more intimate events that create a more conducive environment for building trust and confidence in the participant. You will learn to incorporate a combination of educational events, client appreciation events, focus groups, specialty and image-enhancing events that will work together to grow your practice. You will learn to capitalize on your events to build alliances with other centers of influence. To achieve these results, you must create a multi-tiered program, addressing even non-financial issues, using a multitude of venues and methods that appeal to every gender, age, and preference. By going beyond the simply financial concerns, you enhance your ability to connect with participants in a way that dissolves the traditional stockbroker image.

The seminar program you are about to develop will meet all the needs of the 21st century financial advisor. The framework for your program will stem from your specialization or "tribal market," driven by client needs and issues. You'll tap into your resources of products and services, as well as develop outside alliances to extend your reach even further. Your events will not only be a resource for education, but will greatly enhance the value you bring to your clients, ultimately elevating your client service and ability to generate referrals. Your event program will bolster your marketing efforts and enhance your standing in the community, reinforce your image as a wealth manager, and strengthen your relationship with your clients; all while attracting more business, gathering more assets and having FUN. What could be better than that?

> **Your event program will**
> - **Bolster your marketing efforts**
> - **Enhance your standing in the community**
> - **Reinforce your image as a wealth manager**
> - **Strengthen your relationship with your clients**
> - **Attract more business, gathering more assets**

**What you learned:**
- **In the 1990's seminars created a more efficient method of getting in front of more people.**
- **The one overriding factor that can create the desire and interest to move accounts is the <u>service and value you provide</u>.**
- **Seminars allow you to find new clients and grow your business while increasing client service.**
- **An effective seminar program is the thread that weaves all your marketing efforts together.**
- **Your event program will**
  - **Bolster your marketing efforts**
  - **Enhance your standing in the community**
  - **Reinforce your image as a wealth manager**
  - **Strengthen your relationship with your clients**
  - **Attract more business, gathering more assets**

# Chapter 2
## Step 1: A Multi-Tiered System

**What you will learn:**

- The many different types of events
- How to determine which event is right for your practice
- The importance of your venue
- The foundation to all of your decisions
- The difference between Workshops and Events
- Why Seminars can be difficult
- How to use Cluster Lunches
- The best approach for a Focus Group
- How events are the foundation to your marketing strategy
- What is the best combination of events
- The critical factors to a successful event program
- How your tribal market fits in

The purpose of this chapter is to help you recognize the unique differences of each type of event. You will learn the most important factors that can affect the success of your events and how your events can become the foundation to your overall marketing strategy.

Not all events are the same. Each style of event is unique in its ability to achieve your objectives. Each fills a different role, whether adding greater value to your current clients, generating new clients, or enhancing your image in the community. There are many factors in planning your events that can influence the results. Understanding how each of these factors affects the overall success is critical to building an effective event program. Size, venue and environment all play an important role in the planning phase.

The size of the event is one of the more defining characteristics. Events can range from hundreds of participants to just five; neither being more advantageous than the other is, until you identify your objective. Certainly, a large event lacks the intimacy of an event with five to ten participants and can cause the advisor tremendous anxiety trying to fill a large number of seats. With a large room, acoustics become a critical component as does seating arrangements and of course, the registration. All of this requires extra attention. Although a large event requires more planning and organization, it can also be a great opportunity to enhance your image and level of professionalism.

> **The size of your event is one of the most important factors to your planning.**

A smaller event, usually between five and thirty participants, limits your exposure in the sense that you are not in front of as many new people, but it can be much less stressful AND more productive. Again, all of this depends on your objective. In today's environment, where trust is a rare commodity, the intimate nature of smaller events can create more opportunities to start building the foundation to trusting relationships. Although with small events you eliminate some of the organization and preparation necessary for a larger one, you must still pay particular attention to the details. Because there is more opportunity to engage with your guests, it is important that you adjust the room and your process accordingly. Again, we must go back to your objectives to determine what size event would be the most appropriate.

> **Your overall objective for the events must be the overriding factor in making any decisions.**

The venue is another factor that can change or impact the results. A venue sets a tone that can entice greater attendance or deter participants. The objective and size of your event will help you determine the appropriate setting. Venues can range from restaurants, public facilities and meetings halls, sporting facilities, museums, gardens to boardrooms. The choices are limitless until you narrow it down to the interests of your target market and the objective of your event.

I mentioned interest for a reason. Depending on your target market, you can select a venue that would be of greater interest than other settings might provide. For example, in my early days as an FA, I had the volunteer list to Sherman Gardens, a botanical garden that also had a nice restaurant. Based on my mailing list (Around 150 people), for my very first event, I hosted a luncheon at the botanical gardens focusing on socially aware investing. I had a great turn out, between thirty and forty guests. My purpose for this event was to gain exposure and build my professional reputation. I achieved that objective.

Some venues are more conducive to networking , some are best for serving meals while others are designed for public speaking. The objective for some events is to create open communication between the participants, while others focus more on the core presentation.

Be careful with outdoor events. Depending on the setting, the sound can be challenging. There is nothing worse than attending a presentation and struggling to hear the speaker. When in doubt, even the slightest doubt, USE A MICROPHONE.

> **Your venue must be determined by your objective, tribal market and style of presentation.**

Once you've determined the size and venue, consider the environment. Just because the room is the right size does not mean it will create the right environment for a fruitful event. Many factors affect the environment. The decorations, furniture, the set up of the room, carpets or not, table clothes or not, stadium seating, classroom style or a U-shaped arrangement, all set a tone and create a unique atmosphere. The sound system, the flow of people, and the ability to create privacy are all important factors to consider. Participant positioning, the seat assignment, the size of the tables, the location of the buffet, coffee or appetizers, even the spacing between seats can have an impact on your event.

Again, the environment should be determined first by your target market and second by the objective you want to achieve. My target market was wealthy women in Newport Beach California, aged fifty and above. (For those that watch the TV show the OC, that's where I built my business.) Those women would not be as comfortable in a library conference room, lecture hall or even a local diner. I held most of my events at a five star restaurant, The Ritz in Newport Beach. On the other hand, people not accustomed to this fine dining environment might be a little intimidated, causing them to be more reserved. Not the feeling I was hoping to achieve. Sometimes, you can CREATE an environment or enhance the environment to add more value to your event. For example...

- **Seating:** When guests are spread out and there is too much space between participants, you lose energy in the room. But, when participants are seated shoulder to shoulder, you will find the energy escalates along with the noise level.
- **Room Selection:** When selecting a room, it is better to choose a room that has the potential for being too small vs. too large. It is always better to add tables and chairs at the last minute then to have empty tables or seats. Too large a room can destroy any chance of achieving good interaction with and between the guests.
- **A Packed Room** generates tremendous energy and validates the participants' decision to attend.
- **Greeting your Guests:** Be certain to set up your room so that you can personally engage the participants. It starts the moment they arrive. How you greet your

guests and then introduce them to others can have a tremendous impact on setting the tone for the actual presentation.

- **Assigned seating:** By assigning seats, you are better able to control the environment and the flow of conversation. A great client sitting next to a perspective client enhances your reputation, as most clients love to brag about their advisors.
- **Where you sit:** If you are not the main speaker, sit with your guests, take notes during the presentation and share your notes at the end of the event. This process helps you connect better with your guests, making them feel as if you are also one of them.

> **Depending on your tribal market, you can alter the environment utilizing the following strategies:**
> - **Seating**
> - **Room Selection**
> - **A Packed Room**
> - **Greeting your Guests**
> - **Assigned seating**
> - **Where you sit**

In this program, we will be focusing on five specific types of face-to-face gatherings. They utilize the characteristics listed above in a variety of combinations, making it easier for you to determine which type of program would be most effective in meeting your objective. The five gatherings are:

1. Workshops
2. Events
3. Seminars
4. Cluster Lunches
5. Focus Groups

## Workshops:

Workshops are educational style meetings designed to be facilitative. There can be three to 20 individuals in a casual setting, creating a classroom environment. This is a roll-up-your-sleeves, interactive event. The more interactive you make it; the more effective it will be in generating new accounts. Workshops tend to attract more serious investors, investors that don't need the enticement of a good meal or new experience to attend. A good workshop can become a repeatable event, something you host on a regular basis. These become "feeder" events, great for those people who are just beginning a relationship with you.

> **Workshops are educational style and can be highly effective in generating new accounts.**

Invitations for workshops tend to be less formal. Invites might even include "What you will learn:" sections, so the guests are more prepared to participate. You can send pre-work to the participants, a worksheet that asks questions, reading material or a checklist of items to bring with them. This pre-work reaffirms their commitment to attend, enhances your value and level of professionalism and better prepares the participant, which elevates the whole event.

Typically, workshops are not centered on a meal, but light refreshments can be provided. The participants are there to learn, not to be entertained. A conference room is highly appropriate for a workshop, creating a more classroom-like environment. As participants arrive, you can have them sign in and distribute worksheets or PowerPoint notes. I prefer worksheets designed to be filled out during the presentation, complimenting the topic at hand.

In a workshop, it is important to set the tone early on. You can do this by asking the participants what they hope to learn at the event. Be sure to write everything they say on a flip chart. Although you have an agenda for the evening, odds are many of the statements will fall in line with what you plan to present. It is very important that when the formal presentation is over, you bring the attention back to the flip chart and cross off each item that was addressed. If something wasn't addressed, ask permission to talk to the participant one on one. This process helps to ensure your participants leave the event satisfied they received what they came for.

Providing quizzes and fun learning tools can help create a more open environment. Start off with games like "Investor Jeopardy," ask investment trivia questions or even give a short quiz about the markets to help them realize what they need to learn.

> **Workshops can be fun and interactive. Quizzes and games are effective tools in setting the tone for workshops.**

Getting the participants to interact with each other is critical to creating a facilitative environment. I prefer to either set up my tables in a U-shape or place the chairs in a crescent formation. This allows all of the participants to see each other as they speak and encourages discussion.

The U-shape allows you, the presenter, to walk inside the U, creating a little more intimacy than if you stayed in front of the room. Often, I sit or lean on the end of the table, creating a less formal stance.

Flip charts, white boards and even chocolate coins are valuable tools for these particular events. The intimacy and facilitative nature makes workshops one of the most effective events in getting the participants to take action.

Most workshops include worksheets as well as time during the event for the participants to consider their situation.

## Events:

Formal Events are intimate like a workshop, yet with a more prestigious setting. Like a formal dinner party, events can be promoted as, "exclusive," and should be no more than thirty participants, preferably less. I tend to favor ten to fifteen guests. This number creates good energy, maintains the level of intimacy while better leveraging your time and energy.

> **Events are smaller, more intimate events and typically held in a more formal setting.**

For an event to be effective, it is best when there is a commonality between the participants. For example, they may share a place of work, career, status in life, or even hobby. This commonality makes it easier when introducing the guests to each other. The FA can indicate the mutual interest between the guests, which immediately starts a conversation. In addition, when the guests all have something in common you are better able to focus your thoughts, energy and conversation.

I'll never forget the one time I posted my event in the free calendar section of the newspaper. Most of my guests were from specific mailing lists in Newport Beach. The one guest who learned about the event from the paper had little or nothing in common with my other guests. This difference had a very negative impact on the environment and the willingness of the participants to share their stories. Not only that, but it was more difficult for me to shift gears and converse naturally with this new participant. This is why it is so very important that those you are inviting have some commonality in their lives.

> **Social etiquette is an important to creating a successful environment at your events.**

Events usually center on a meal, and can be held at a local restaurant or catered in your branch conference room. At my last event as a financial advisor, I had the lunch served at the top of the green at an exclusive golf resort. Although this was an outside event, we were alone on the green under a tent. Because there were only ten or fifteen guests, the sound quality was excellent. It was a wonderful event.

More often than not, formal events are held in a restaurant. It's helpful if you can reserve a private room, so there are few if any distractions. This also creates a sense of confidentiality and exclusivity. Remember, even the private room should be smaller than you need. When you must add more tables and chairs, the energy escalates with the increase in bodies. Being over crowded is a great problem. The increase in attendance tends to validate the participants desire to attend the event. (See Chapter 6 for choosing an appropriate restaurant.)

Choosing an event location provides an opportunity for tremendous creativity – golf courses, wine cellars or museums. Perhaps you have a beautiful home or a large boat for entertaining. These personally owned venues have an even greater impact on the guests.

Most events will feature you and/or a guest presenter, with a focus on a product, service, process or perhaps just an opportunity to thank your clients for their business. Formal events are often the most appropriate choice for client appreciation programs.

> **Be creative with the venue for events, focusing on the interest of your tribal market.**

## Event as a Strategy

Jody McGovern, a financial consultant, moved her practice from Pennsylvania to Georgia. Though many of her clients transferred with her, Jody knew she was going to have to become more visible in her new community. With that in mind, Jody developed a monthly "Women and Wealth" program. Each month, she focuses on a specific topic, with the participants paying for their own lunch. Jody's presentations focus on subjects relevant to her target market and she often invites specialists to discuss their area of expertise.

Today, Jody has more than thirty participants at each luncheon. She is now adding additional events to accommodate the increase in attendees. In a relatively short time, Jody has developed a long list of qualified prospects and has made herself known as the financial advisor of choice for women in her new community.

## Seminars:

Large seminars enhance your image in the community. They usually have from fifty to one hundred or more participants. This is not an intimate setting, so your message must be well prepared and orchestrated. They can be used as initiator, appreciation, or specialty event. Many seminars focus on non-financial as well as financial issues of interest to your tribal market. Specialists from outside the financial services industry can be invited to speak, and if presented properly, allow you to tap into the client base of the presenter as well.

> **Seminars can enhance your image in the community.**

As the host of a large seminar, you must be free to mingle and converse with the guests; therefore, you must have a team of support staff to manage the details of the event. Having a reception table, an alphabetized roster of participants and assigned seating are all important components of a well- orchestrated seminar. Remember, from the moment your guests walk through the door, you want to be certain their experience reflects their experience as your client.

I am not a strong proponent of large seminars; therefore, we will not spend much time addressing the nuances of seminars. In my experience, I have found that smaller, more intimate client gatherings provided the best response in my target market.

If your objective is to open more accounts, workshops and events tend to be the most effective methods in getting appointments and commitments from the participants. However, if you are looking to gain more public exposure, be introduced to new prospective clients, or enhance your image within the community, seminars may be your most productive program. I encourage you to test each type of client gathering to determine how your target market responds.

## Cluster Lunches:

Cluster lunches are smaller than an event, less formal and with a bit of a workshop feel. A cluster lunch is an opportunity to bring together clients and or prospects with a specific purpose in mind. Sometimes, that purpose could be to give you feedback regarding your service and value. Perhaps the topic is an investment that is exclusive to particular kinds of investors. A cluster lunch could also be to celebrate a special occasion or a client's birthday. Often notes are taken, either by you (as you are learning what you could be doing better) or by the participants, as they learn about a new product or process. Although it's preferable to have a private room, it's not as necessary, as long as you can find a quiet table with little to no foot traffic around it.

Again, just like with all our programs, you must be clear on your objective. Your guests may perceive the event to have one objective, to gain their feedback and ideas. Your objective may be quite different. Your purpose may be to leave the meeting with two new appointments. In this situation, you must be very strategic in how you move from what they perceive as the object to what you truly intend. A smooth transition is critical but highly effective. Even a birthday celebration can have two objectives. The birthday guest perceives a gift of appreciation while your objective may be to get yourself introduced to three or four friends of your best client. Your client walks away with increased loyalty, you walk away with three new potential leads and the other guests walk away wondering, "Why doesn't my advisor do that for me?"

> **A Cluster Lunch can have two primary objectives: yours and what the participants perceive to be the objective.**

## Focus Group:

Think of a focus group like a cluster lunch with a few more participants and in a bit more of a structured setting. In my practice, once my client (the financial advisor) has redesigned their business model and marketing message, it is critical that ALL of his or her clients learn the new message and model. Sending a letter does little justice to the work put into creating this practice. Therefore, you want to get face to face with all of your best clients.

Giving them a one-on-one presentation can create too much pressure on the recipient. In a focus group, not only are you better able to leverage your time and energy, but you create a "club" like atmosphere, enhancing feedback and conversation. In addition, if designed properly, you can sprinkle some new prospective clients into the group. During the focus group, those prospective clients realize the value you provide and the lack of service they are receiving from their current environment.

As with any of these events, the focus group has a clearly defined objective for both the guests as well as the FA. The guests are invited with the understanding that you have redesigned your business model and, as their opinion and advice is important to you, you want to present it to them face to face. It is rare that this request is refused, unless there is a schedule conflict.

As for the prospects, you can mention to your client that to gain a more objective opinion it is valuable that a few non-clients are there so that we can learn what other advisors are doing and not doing. Your client is encouraged to suggest a friend or associate that might be a good addition to the group. You can go through your contact list, prospect pipeline, or even Christmas card mailing list and find individuals you would like to impress. This is a great opportunity to give a prospective client that final PUSH.

The blend of clients and prospects adds to the opportunity to gain valuable feedback and for the non-clients to get a good understanding of what you do. Your objective is that your clients walk away energized and impressed with the message, organization and value you provide them, and the non-clients walk away scratching their heads thinking, "What is my advisor doing for me?" This process enhances their ability to refer you to others. This same feeling and impact could never be obtained from a letter.

> **A focus group is an effective method to present your value to both clients and prospects.**

Now, before we end this piece on focus groups, it is absolutely critical that I clarify the difference between what I call focus groups and what others call "advisory groups." Many coaching companies out there suggest you develop an advisory group as part of the process of redesigning your practice. This is a group of clients (I have yet to hear of prospects being included) who are asked to provide ongoing feedback in order to help you improve your practice. I have a problem with this.

Clients only know what they know. They typically will only suggest what they have already experienced so it would be a rare experience for a client to give you a really out of the box idea that could change the way you do business. The objective of these traditional advisory groups is to let your clients provide you with ideas that you could implement.

That is why I prefer my clients host focus groups. You see, I believe YOU know what the client wants and have a better understanding as to what you can do to WOW the client to give you referrals.

Nine times out of ten, when my clients (FA's) present their new business model, their clients are amazed at how well the FA recognized what they want and need in advance. They are impressed with the enhanced level of service their FA plans to provide, that they would have never thought of themselves.

Another point of contention, whereas you will typically meet with the same advisory group a few times a year, you can create as many focus groups as you want. This allows you to penetrate deep into your book. Your intent is that every one of your clients recognizes your message, your model and more importantly the incredible value you intend to deliver. This knowledge is the foundation for generating referrals.

> **Come to your event KNOWING what the client needs and wants.**

## The Ultimate Combination

Most of you will be thinking about one of these programs as the event of choice for you and your target market. I don't want you to narrow your thoughts to just one event. A combination of events has the greatest impact.

Once you set up your initial events, they become easily repeatable, saving you time and energy. Also, this repetition enhances your marketing ability (we will talk more about this later in the book).

Now that you understand the purpose of the different events, workshops, seminars, focus groups and cluster lunches. Your next step is developing a combination of events that can leverage all we've talked about in a way that has the greatest impact on you and the growth of your business.

What do I mean by a combination? As we will discuss in the next chapter, your topics should be based on the three core needs of your target market. Select two financial needs and one softer, more personal issue.

For example, you might have one topic addressed in monthly workshops held in your branch office, address another issue through a monthly or quarterly formal event at a local restaurant, and incorporate a larger seminar annually that addresses the softer issues that tend to attract a larger audience. This integrated method should be designed around your comfort level, how many events you can handle, what is appropriate for your target market, and which combination will allow you to have the greatest impact on your clients and prospects.

Now, don't get excited or anxious. I'll show you exactly how to do all this. You can take it one simple step at a time. For now, just embrace this multi-tiered process and accept that it is important to your practice.

> **It's a combination of events that has the greatest impact on growing your business.**

This was my ultimate combination when I was an active FA: I held a branch workshop on a monthly basis, a money manager event at the Ritz on a quarterly basis, and a seminar (30+ guests) once or twice a year. (I would often partner up with another FA to make the seminar even larger and limit my level of seat filling.) Certainly, there can be variations to this plan, but I've found this process to be the most functional for a number of reasons.

Workshops, because of their less formal, educational structure take less time, preparation and typically cost less, which reduces stress. The FA is usually the presenter, so the planning is less complicated than coordinating with a guest speaker. The intimacy and classroom environment makes your office conference room an ideal location; and with limited beverages, your cost can be minimal. All of these factors make workshops the most feasible events to hold on a monthly basis.

Another factor that can make workshops effective and easy is to repeat the topic. Let me clarify. Think of your workshops as your feeder event. If you hold one every month, focusing on the same topic, all of your clients can market this for you year round. This could be a great opportunity for you to be introduced to potential clients and referrals. Because of the intimate and conversational nature of these events, you are better able to learn whether a participant truly qualifies for your practice.

Next are formal events. Because they are more exclusive, they may take a bit more coordination at first. I say at first because once you have the routine down, the process become effortless. It is for this reason that I recommend you find a venue that works and stick to it. Once you have a great restaurant, you will be familiar with the staff and all the details.

Allow yourself plenty of time between formal events so that you can be creative and unique. In that way, each formal event will be special and attractive to clients. You can find unique venues, topics, and speakers, without creating too much pressure on you and your team. But again, don't make more work for yourself; if you find a venue that works and is attractive to your target market, take advantage of it. Get to know the staff and ensure they get to know you. This has a tremendous impact on the flow of the event. In addition, just like the consistency of the workshops, a regular venue adds to your clients' ability to anticipate and market your next event for you.

> **Making your events repeatable is critical to the process.**

## Give Yourself Time

Large Seminars, due to their size and hopefully unique topic, can be the most challenging events in regards to time, money, and coordination. Therefore, you must be certain that you design the event to meet the needs of your target market, add tremendous value to the participants, enhance your ability to attract new prospects and clients, and be repeatable so that each year you are not re-inventing the wheel. Seminars require the most planning and preparation.

Due to of the size of these events, they can also create additional stress and anxiety. This is why I always partnered with at least one additional FA. Because you are initiating the seminar, you get to be the host and make the introductions (this is important), but because you are sharing the event, you can break down the responsibilities and spread the seating so that you are only responsible for filling X number of seats. For an event of this type, be sure to give yourself at least six months to prepare.

## The Annual Event

A former coaching client of mine sponsors "The Annual Client University." At the beginning of every year, they host a full-day event focusing on a multitude of issues specific to their target market. They use both internal specialists and external speakers to address some of the softer issues.

This past year my former client had more than 300 participants at their seminar. More importantly, there were a large number of attorneys and CPA's who attended and brought clients. The consistency of this seminar allows these financial advisors to add it to their marketing brochure and provides a fabulous marketing vehicle, not to mention a full pipeline of new prospects each year.

This is a great example of how to consistently generate a large following and elevate your image in the community. However, this type of program can take tremendous time, energy, and coordination of resources. Don't attempt this event without a lot of planning, preparation and additional employees to share the responsibilities

## Tribal Marketing:

Now, let's put it all together, starting with the tribal market. During my time as an FA in Newport Beach, I had a clearly defined target market: women over fifty. I had a real understanding of their core needs and issues.

Many of these women were already responsible for managing their financial lives, yet lacked the knowledge and more importantly the confidence to make sound financial decisions. Needless to say, most were not savvy investors, and had relied on a husband, brother, father, and even son, to help make their financial decisions. These women had a desire to become more involved, but were uncomfortable with their lack of knowledge, which dramatically affected their confidence and deterred them from getting more involved.

My goal was not simply to educate these women. It was to increase their confidence and encourage their involvement in finance by making it enjoyable, while providing them with the highest level of professional management.

With this in mind, I developed the following multi-tiered program:

- **Monthly Workshops** focusing on investing 101. This informal setting allowed my clients and prospects to become more comfortable with me. They learned the fundamentals of investing, while asking more personal questions they would not ask in a more formal environment. I created a warm, comfortable atmosphere that encouraged these women to open up and express their issues and concerns without feeling embarrassed or chastised.
- **Monthly Events:** In coordination with my workshops and specialty events, I consistently held a monthly event focusing on professional money managers. This topic not only further educated my clients, it allowed them

to become more comfortable with the professional management I would recommend. I also opened this event up to men as well as women, which allowed many women the opportunity to introduce me to their husbands, fathers and sons who were also involved in their financial decision making. I learned that by being introduced to their male "mentor," it became much easier to open accounts with these women. I was amazed at how many men wanted their wives and mothers to become more engaged in their financial affairs and now saw my practice as the vehicle to learn. Surprisingly, although my target market was women, I had many couples and even single men as clients after initiating these monthly co-ed gatherings.

- **Quarterly Formal Events:** These events were designed specifically to focus on the needs and concerns of these women beyond the realm of finance. My intent was to create some fun with money matters. My hope was to help them recognize that investing incorporated many of the same concepts they used in other aspects of their lives. Health, beauty, and fashion were all popular topics and allowed me to partner with other professionals for these "specialty women's" events. These events were also particularly effective in generating new leads. I encouraged my clients to invite a new friend to attend. The topics made this process even easier. And sharing an event with another professional adds the bonus of getting them to market the event with their clients and prospects as well. This is a very valuable concept we will discuss at another time.

- **Annual Seminar:** This event was designed to attract new prospects, featuring a topic that combined finance with a hot topic relevant to the times and my target market. The seminar was a good opportunity to initiate a new mailing list into my event program. How I approached this event was entirely different than all my others. I really wanted to get in front of lots of new people.

**NOTE:** *Don't feel pressured to host an annual large seminar unless an idea presents itself that makes it easy. The stress, level of organization and planning necessary can make seminars counterproductive to growing the business.*

The most important aspect of my program was that it met the specific needs of my target market – education, professional management, and confidence. Also important was the consistency of my events, allowing my clients to plan ahead and market my events to others. It was not uncommon for me to receive a phone call from a client asking if she could bring three friends or family members to an event the following month.

Before you start planning, you must remember the importance of consistency. **This may be the most important concept when planning your events.**

Do you remember when the show American Idol first came out? Everyone was talking about it. Perhaps you even scheduled your evening around the show and spent the following day discussing it with friends, co-workers, and family. It's true of any favorite show. Because of the consistency and regularity – same day every week, same time, and same channel – American Idol becomes part of your routine. What if they were to randomly skip a month or week? Would you continue watching? Would you continue talking about it? Would it have the same residual value? No. You could no longer depend on the program. Your event process is no different.

A critical component to this whole seminar process is consistency. Most financial advisors who have failed with seminars lacked consistency and held their events on a random basis.

Random events can be a one-time affair or a few events sprinkled in throughout the year with little to no connection or theme. Because of their inconsistent nature, clients and prospects never know when the next event will be or what you will be discussing. Clients are unable to plan ahead or bring a friend, because they don't know what to expect or when it will happen next.

Whether you have just one type of event each year or develop a multi-tiered strategy, the continuity and consistency of your program will be one of the most critical aspects to your success. Without this consistency, you limit your marketability. You can NOT advertise or present this "random" event as part of your service or value. Without consistency, you deny yourself more than half of the value of hosting events all together.

If you have a monthly event, be sure to host it on a specific week, day, or time. If you have quarterly events, be consistent. If you hold an annual event, make it something your clients and prospects think is special enough to reserve on their calendars in advance.

For example, if you are planning a monthly workshop, hold it in your branch office on the third Thursday of every month. Market the recurring program, perhaps calling it the "Third Thursday Workshop," or, "Women's Wealth Wednesday." A clever title adds to your ability to market both yourself and your events.

When you are consistent, clients and prospects will grow to depend on your events and know they are always at a certain time, day, and location. This makes it easier for them to promote it to other prospective clients they meet.

> **The continuity and consistency of your program will be one of the most critical aspects of your success.**

Once you have established a consistent event program with regularly scheduled events, you can begin marketing. In order to better leverage this event program, I recommend you create an event calendar. This calendar allows you to see and plan three months in advance. By doing this, you are better able to plan your budget, coordinate campaigns tied to your event topics, and schedule time away from the office.

In a later chapter, I will show you how to spruce up your calendar so that you can send it out to your clients and prospects, thereby providing them advance notice of upcoming opportunities. This advance notice increases their tendency to share the information with others.

There is one more benefit to planning your events three months in advance. Once you have committed to your calendar, you are more apt to stay focused and energized, knowing you have a room to fill with clients and prospects.

Then, once one event is over, you must immediately begin promoting and marketing your next one. In fact, one of the greatest benefits of advanced planning is the opportunity to announce your next event at the close of your latest one, and get the buzz going early.

> **Developing your event calendar is the foundation to your marketing strategy.**

You know, there is one more reason that events are an effective method for growing your business. You have a good reason to talk to people.

Just like an invitation in the mail can spark the interest of a stranger, so too can a verbal invitation over the phone. Whether we are cold calling, cold walking, networking or hosting events, our immediate objective is to open the dialogue and start a conversation.

So many FA's have lost sight of the important opportunity that comes from hosting an event. Instead of taking advantage of this opening, they call or have an intern call strictly to get an RSVP. In most cases, the conversations are very brief, generating a yes/no answer.

However, if you recognize this invite as an opportunity to develop a relationship, then this quick, unobtrusive personal call can turn into a fabulous opportunity to engage in conversation, begin the process of developing a rapport, while profiling and qualifying this person as appropriate for your business.

There were many times when making calls for one event, I would suggest another event of mine after I learned the prospect's level of assets and sophistication. The point of this is, don't call on events just to get a yes or no answer. Leverage these calls to open the door to a new and productive relationship. The event then becomes the bonus.

> **Marketing your events creates opportunities to enter into dialogue with clients and prospects.**

The benefits of a consistent event program are truly unlimited if properly planned, marketed, and executed.

To fully realize the impact of this program, I recommend a combination of events that will allow you to better leverage your efforts and enhance your marketability. This three-tiered program may seem daunting to you now, but remember this isn't something you jump into all at once. I designed this book is so you can build on your process with a strategic plan in mind. Your three-tiered program will start small and build over time, each step building a strong foundation for the next step in the process.

**What you learned:**

- The size of your event is one of the most important factors to your event program.
- Your overall objective for the events must be the overriding factor in making any decisions.
- Your venue must be determined by your objective, tribal market and style of presentation.
- Depending on your tribal market, you can alter the environment utilizing the following strategies:
    - Seating
    - Room Selection
    - A Packed Room
    - Greeting your Guests
    - Assigned seating
    - Where you sit
- Workshops are educational in style and can be highly effective in generating new accounts.
- Workshops can be fun and interactive. Quizzes and Games are effective tools in setting the tone for workshops.
- Events are smaller more intimate events and are typically held in a more formal setting.
- Social etiquette is important to creating a successful environment at your events.
- Be creative with the venue for events focusing on the interest of your tribal market.
- Seminars can enhance your image in the community.
- An effective seminar requires a dependable and experienced staff.
- A cluster lunch can have two primary objectives: yours and what the participants perceives as the objective.
- A focus group is an effective method to present your value to both clients and prospects.
- Come to your event KNOWING what the client needs and wants.
- A combination of events has the greatest impact on growing your business.
- Making your events repeatable is critical to the process.

- **It all starts with your Tribal Market.**
- **An effective event program must meet the specific needs of your tribal market.**
- **The continuity and consistency of your program will be one of the most critical aspects of your success.**
- **Developing your event calendar is the foundation to your marketing strategy.**
- **Marketing your events creates opportunities to enter into dialogue with clients and prospects.**

# Assignment #1

On Worksheet A, in the following page, develop the seminar structure that makes sense for you. Initially, this program will demand some extra time and energy, but once the foundation is developed and the systems are in place, you'll have a platform to build on. You can always add on later. So for now, create the model that will help you develop your long-term practice.

1. Start with your monthly event. If you plan to give a workshop every month, pencil in "workshop" in the first row. At this point, just pencil it in for each month. We will be going back and eliminating any conflicts due to other events and holidays.
2. Next, focus on events. Determine the best months for your events and pencil them in.
3. If you plan to hold a seminar, which month would generate the greatest amount of participation? Pencil it in the third row.
4. Go back through your schedule, checking holiday months, as well as where you have too much overlap, and pare it down to a manageable level.

It's important to note that July and August tend to be challenging months for events. Keep that in mind while as you schedule.

## Example of a Preliminary Planner

| JANUARY | FEBRUARY | MARCH | APRIL | MAY |
|---------|----------|-------|-------|-----|
| Workshop | Workshop | Workshop | Workshop | Workshop |
| Event | | | | Event |
| | | Seminar | | |

# WORKSHEET A

## Preliminary Planner

| JANUARY | FEBRUARY | MARCH |
|---|---|---|
| | | |
| | | |
| | | |

| APRIL | MAY | JUNE |
|---|---|---|
| | | |
| | | |
| | | |

| JULY | AUGUST | SEPTEMBER |
|---|---|---|
| | | |
| | | |
| | | |

| OCTOBER | NOVEMBER | DECEMBER |
|---|---|---|
| | | |
| | | |
| | | |

# Chapter 3

## Step 2: Make it Market Driven

**What you will learn:**

- **What is Tribal Marketing**
- **Why tribal marketing is important**
- **How tribal marketing affects my event program**
- **The benefits of tribal marketing**

Before we can move forward to the next step, it is imperative that you understand the importance of tribal marketing. No, that wasn't a typo. I have always been a big believer in "target" marketing and have always applied it in my many sales positions. In my coaching and training, however I have found most FA's highly resistant to the concept. Although intellectually they seem to recognize the value, there seems to be a chasm between agreeing to the concept and actually applying it.

I was introduced to the concept of tribal marketing by Dave Logan and John King in their book Tribal Leadership. Where target marketing has evolved into an over-taught redundant concept, tribal marketing helps to bring the concept home. Tribal marketing helps us to embrace the importance of the "niche" concept and validates the need for its application.

So, what is tribal marketing?

Think of a tribe as a group of people who naturally gravitate to one another based on a commonality. It could be your status in life, your religion or beliefs. A tribe is a group of people with whom you feel comfortable, at ease, and accepted.

This is the same feeling we are trying to create in your business. If you prospect individuals that would naturally be a part of your tribe, the process becomes easier, almost effortless. The clients become more loyal than those you struggled to accept. When you can identify your tribe and your tribal market, you will naturally have a better understanding of the challenges they experience, the things that are important to them and the solutions that appeal to them.

So, why is this concept of tribal marketing so important when talking about seminars?

Probably the most common mistake of all seminars is they are not driven by the needs and interests of a tribal market. So much of the time, we focus on what we think our clients and prospects should be interested in, and not what they actually are interested in. Because of this attitude, many financial advisors have had less than successful events. If we can communicate our understanding of what is important to our market, we are better able to attract their attention and interest.

> **The needs and issues of your tribal market must drive your events.**

## Have You Sworn Off Seminars?

During a presentation I gave to a large group of financial advisors, a participant adamantly voiced his opinion that seminars were a complete waste of time and energy. He shared with the group that he had spent a tremendous amount of time, energy, and money preparing a financial planning seminar. After three attempts, he had yet to open an account after his events. He considered seminars a losing proposition.

It was obvious this financial advisor had good public speaking skills and had spoken to groups before. He knew cold calling wasn't working for him, and he had less time to spend on it. He wanted to leverage his strengths and his time so seminars seemed like the perfect solution.

Considering his natural ability as a public speaker, I needed to gather more information to determine the cause of his poor results. I asked him some specific questions about his failed seminars:

**Adri:** When planning the first event, what was the first thing you did?

**Fred:** I went online to find a seminar that I thought was relevant to my process and that I felt comfortable in presenting. I found a retirement planning seminar that I felt would apply to everyone who attended.

What was his first mistake?

_____

_____

_____

**Adri:** Who did you invite to this event?

**Fred:** One of the local mutual fund wholesalers offered me a lead list of 2000 individuals with $500,000 in investment assets. Then I found a local restaurant to hold my event. It was just around the corner, which would make it easy for me and they had reasonable prices for meals. I created an invitation on my letterhead and used window envelopes to save time and money. Because I had so many invitations, I was able to use bulk mail postage.

What were his next mistakes?

_____

_____

_____

**Adri:** After you sent out the invites, what was your response rate?

**Fred:** I received about seventeen RSVP's, but only ten showed up.

**Adri:** How many of those participants were actually qualified prospects?

**Fred:** Probably only about five.

Thinking it was just bad timing and that things would get better next time, Fred repeated this process twice, with dismal results. No wonder Fred gave up on seminars as a marketing tool.

Unfortunately, Fred's experience with seminars is typical. In fact, most financial advisors have attempted seminars in the same way. I have met hundreds and thousands of financial advisors who have attempted the same thing with miserable results. Unfortunately, Fred was destined to fail from the moment he considered using seminars for his practice. Here are a few of the core issues that derailed his program:

- Fred didn't select his seminar based on his prospect/ clients' primary needs, but what was easiest and the most comfortable seminar for him to present.
- The people in his lead list had nothing in common except that they all had more than $500,000. This actually tells us little about their shared needs and concerns.
- The venue he selected, although appropriate for his checkbook, had little or no appeal to the target market.

- Fred's invitations were not compelling. Probably few prospects even bothered to open the envelope.
- Finally, Fred should have followed up with phone calls on every invitation. Calling those who RSVP'd would have refreshed their commitment to attending the event and help them value it's importance to their financial future.

Large seminars just don't work if you are trying to appeal to a large group of individuals who have different needs, interests, and financial concerns. That's why tribal marketing is so critical to a successful seminar program.

> **Your audience must have similar needs, interests and financial concerns.**

## The Power of Tribal Marketing

The very first step in this process is to select a defined tribal market. There are many reasons why starting with a defined tribal market is absolutely, positively critical to your success.

1. **Meet the need:** Each event should be designed to meet one of the three core needs of your market. If your tribal market is not specific enough, it will be very difficult to zero in on the tribe's hot buttons or primary concerns. It is all too common for the financial advisor to transpose what he/she believes the client or prospect should be losing sleep over, with what is actually keeping them up at night. **And here lies our core responsibility as advisors.** By addressing their concerns first, we create the opportunity to educate and steer our tribe to focus on the fundamental issues that can improve or impede their financial future. By understanding their core issues and concerns, you are better able to design your practice around the solutions to those three issues.

2. **Create good chemistry:** Creating positive synergy at your events depends a great deal on the chemistry of the

participants. When the participants share a status in life, social issues, or profession, for example: older women, business owners, lawyers etc... they immediately feel more comfortable.

3. **Synergistic Marketing:** Remember, the seminar program is an integral part to your master marketing plan. Without it, your practice will be fragmented. All of your marketing materials should be coordinated around the needs and concerns of your tribal market, reiterating and emphasizing the core message, whether through your events, your brochures, or your direct communication with clients and prospects.

---

**An effective event must:**

- **Meet the need**
- **Create good chemistry**
- **Be supported by synergistic Marketing**

---

## A Tribal Market is Not...

Soon, I will ask you to identify your tribal market. It's important that you are clear and specific. I think the best way to explain what I am looking for is to work backwards.

**Not a Tribal market:** Women.

**Tribal market:** Retired Women; female attorneys; female executives; female business owners; widows, and single divorced women just to name a few. The needs and concerns of a retired woman can be vastly different that that of a woman who works in a corporation. The issues that plague a single, divorced woman greatly contrast those of women business owners. By being specific, you are better able to address the needs of your tribal market and attract more ideal clients to your practice.

**Not a tribal market:** Business owners.

**Tribal market:** Business owners with 5-10 employees; business owners with 5 million plus in revenues; business owners in a particular industry; business owners looking to retire. As you can imagine, the core issues of the owner of a small start-up can greatly contrast those of the owner of a well-established company. Even the stage of life of the business owner can greatly alter the focus and emphasis of your marketing message. The business owner who is looking to retire is interested in issues that other business owners haven't even considered. Again, the more specific you are, the better able you are to address the issues relevant to your tribal market.

I hope that you are starting to embrace the importance of tribal marketing. Many of you may hesitate or over time, fall back to your old ways – marketing and prospecting to the masses. Many of you, or perhaps most of you, fail to zero in on a specific target market for fear of denying yourself all the other potential clients. To the contrary, let me assure you that this will not be the case.

Remember, your tribal market defines your marketing strategy. This is not a rule or a policy but a way of attracting the types of clients that you are best suited to working with. Because this process helps your message become clearer, you will not only attract more of your "ideal" clients, but will peak the interest of other potential clients purely because your message is so compelling. In addition, because your message is so targeted, even those who don't become your client will be able to refer clients to you – if only because they remember what you do.

> **Tribal marketing naturally attracts more clients to your practice.**

Recently, I received a call from a former client. Mike originally came to me in his second or third year in production. We worked together for about a year. Although Mike was very coachable and willing to do what it took to succeed, he struggled to see the value in tribal marketing. Today, as he continues to experience lackluster market performance, Mike recognizes he lacks a quality book of business. Mike was great at doing the numbers and bringing in the clients, but his clients were a mixed bag of people with little in common with each other, much less with Mike. As a result, they lacked the loyalty, commitment and desire to stay when the going got tough. Mike now recognizes the importance of defining your tribe and marketing to it.

> **A tribal market creates a more loyal, productive client.**

Another testament to tribal marketing comes from my own experience. When I first started cold calling to build my business, I never hesitated to share that fact that I specialized in helping women with their financial affairs. I shared this fact with both men and women. My passion and commitment to my tribal market encouraged a brand new prospect (male I might add) to refer one of his women friends to me. She had just received over a million dollars. After many referrals, that man eventually became my client as well.

> **Tribal marketing attracts more interest and attention.**

As you consider these examples, remember, the more specific your tribal market the more clarity you will have in identifying their three core issues. In addition, the more specific your tribal market, the easier these assignments will be and the more effective your marketing plan. But if you do not clearly define a specific tribal market, this program WILL NOT WORK.

**What you learned:**

- A tribal market creates a more loyal productive client.
- Tribal marketing naturally attracts more clients to your practice.
- An effective event must:
  - Meet the need
  - Create good chemistry
  - Be supported by synergistic marketing
- Your audience must have similar needs, interests and financial concerns.
- The needs and issues of your tribal market must drive your events.

# Assignment 2

**Worksheet B:** Tribal Market – three core needs

**B-1:** Focusing on one specific tribal market, your first objective is to identify the three primary issues of your market. You may have an idea as to these needs based on experience and tenure, but to know for sure you must go directly to your tribal market. Consider meeting with two or three of your "ideal" clients. Ask for their help in exploring their issues and concerns. Allow them to validate whether or not you are on the right track. Take advantage of this opportunity to learn their expectations of an ideal financial advisor and find topics which would inspire them to attend an event. Remember, they do not all have to be financial concerns.

**B-2:** Once you have identified the primary concerns of your tribal market, change each concern into a need that you can fill. For example, if they are concerned about their lack of knowledge, then education becomes a need. If they are concerned about a looming retirement, a retirement plan may be the need. If their concern is children, estate planning may be the need.

**B-3:** What topics for your seminar program would address each need? Education may focus on investing 101. Estate planning might cater to trusts, long-term care, and so on.

Sample **TRIBAL MARKET:** _____
(Be specific)

| Concerns of Tribal Mkt. | Needs of Tribal Mkt. | Potential Topics | Method |
|---|---|---|---|
| Lacking knowledge | Education | Investing 101 | Monthly workshops |
| Quality trustworthy money management | Separately Managed Accts | Money Managers | Quarterly featuring money managers |
| Confidence in future | Motivation and Inspiration | Health Advice Fitness Advice | Annual Health and Wealth symposium |

**B-4:** Now, based on the core needs and appropriate topics, determine which would be the most viable topics for what types of event. For example, which topic would be relevant for a monthly workshop? Which event would be best presented quarterly and which is better suited as a seminar? Although we are trying to create a yearlong template, we will be working on a quarterly basis and use the remainder of the calendar as a guide that can be adjusted as needs change.

Be sure to complete only the first four columns on Worksheet B

## WORKSHEET B

TARGET MARKET: _____

(Be specific)

| B-1<br>Concerns of Target Mkt. | B-2<br>Needs of Target Mkt. | B-3<br>Potential Topics | B-4<br>Method | B-5<br>Objective |
|---|---|---|---|---|
| | | | | 1.<br><br>2. |
| | | | | 1.<br><br>2. |
| | | | | 1.<br><br>2. |

# Chapter 4
## Step 3: Know your Goal

**What you will learn:**
- **What is a realistic expectation**
- **The importance of a clear objective**
- **Ways to measure your progress**
- **How to develop a master marketing plan**
- **How to use your Event Calendar as a marketing tool**

The purpose of this chapter is to help you recognize the importance of setting clear objectives with realistic expectations. You will learn how to use an event calendar to differentiate yourself from the competition.

Whenever I ask a financial advisor the objective for their upcoming event, the answer is ALWAYS, "To open more accounts." Well, that's the ultimate goal, but it is an unlikely objective for one event. With such lofty aspirations, you will inevitably be disappointed with your results. To think in today's environment that someone will attend your event for the first time and open an account as a result presumes way too much. Your goals for each of your events should be clearly defined and realistic. You must know what you want to achieve. And again, it all goes back to your tribal market.

Once you have identified your tribal market and determined its core needs and concerns, it's time to take a step back and think about what you are trying to achieve. Certainly, we all want to grow our business.

Consider what you want to take away from each event. Are you trying to:

- Sell a product?
- Open a new account?
- Educate your clients and show your appreciation for their business?

Recognizing what you are actually trying to achieve will help keep your events more focused and organized. It will enhance your ability to evaluate and measure your progress. There are just a handful of typical objectives for events:

1. An appointment
2. A referral or introduction
3. Sell a product
4. Increase client loyalty
5. Enhance your value

It is not uncommon to have two objectives, a primary and a secondary. For example, you may hold an appreciation event to generate good will amongst your clients while, at the same time, allowing them the opportunity to bring a guest or potential referral. The key is identifying your primary goal. A common mistake is not identifying your objective and expecting each event to accomplish too many things. This causes you to dilute your efforts and your focus, thereby denying yourself the full benefits of the event.

Let me give you a few examples. Some events' sole purpose might be to get clients to bring friends and associates. That is exactly what Jody McGovern focused on, her first year in Georgia. Her objective was to increase her exposure in the community and develop a full pipeline of prospects. She did just that. Had she tried to sell a product or push for an appointment, she might have become discouraged with the program.

---

**Set realistic expectations for your individual events.**

---

Doug Bruton provides high-end educational events to a prestigious group of friends and associates (his tribal market). His intent is not to sell, but to elevate his status as a provider of solutions within his community.

Keith Schuss, in Ohio, hosts six to ten educational events for attorneys a year. His objective is to grow his lead list and create an opportunity to meet one on one with each of the attorneys.

Bill Stokes held a focus lunch. His objective? To clarify his practice message and business model in the minds of the participants. This clarity would reinforce and support their ability to send him referrals.

All of these advisors were extremely successful in achieving their objectives. Why? First, they clearly defined their objective and second, their objective was realistic.

## Are You Willing to Measure Your Progress?

Defining a clear and realistic objective also gives you the opportunity and ability to measure your progress. It can be difficult to tell where you are when you're not sure where you're going. Because these advisors knew exactly what they wanted to achieve, they were able to objectively measure results by determining how many new participants were exposed to their practice and how many new leads/prospects were added to their databases.

Remember, not all events generate business on the day. Had these advisors measured their progress by how many accounts they opened, which was not their objective, they may have become greatly discouraged early on, denying themselves further opportunities to develop a successful program.

> **By defining a clear objective, you are able to measure your progress.**

Some events are designed specifically to introduce and sell a new product. Although Doug Bruton hosted high-end educational events from time to time, he would also hold events promoting a specific investment or professional manager. He was very clear, even with his guests, what the objective was. He was very successful in opening accounts with this process. Again, his objectives were clearly defined as well as realistic.

Alternative investment events, money manager events, and annuity programs, are all commonly used product-driven events. The objective is to get the participant to invest in or to commit to a product or service. Therefore, your sales numbers determine your results.

How you present your information will make all the difference as to whether you get the participants to take action. How you introduce and close the event will vary depending on your objective. You cannot provide the same presentation format and hope to get different results.

Educational events can be very effective in elevating client loyalty and promoting your service and value to prospects or potential clients. Presenting an economist, community leader, or professional speaker to provide value can be an effective tool that increases loyalty and sets the stage for introductions. Although client loyalty is difficult to quantify, overtime and with repeated events you can measure the number of guests your clients are bringing to the events. In this situation, the primary objective is client loyalty with the secondary being referrals.

## Adding value

Let's take another look at Doug Bruton's events. As a financial advisor in Texas, he spent the past year targeting the ultra high net worth in his community. He wanted to create a series of events, held six times a year, featuring a public official, the CEO of a major corporation, and a variety of other high profile speakers (not necessarily in the financial industry) which would be of interest to his entrepreneurial target market.

Doug knew that individuals with substantial assets do not make decisions overnight; therefore, his objective was to develop a relationship over time with the participants and create an image of adding value to his clients.

> **Your objectives can be both long term as well as immediate.**

Early on, Doug recognized his tribal market and recognized the issues which concerned them. It was this understanding that guided Doug in his ability to bring highly desired presenters to events that attracted a number of high net worth entrepreneurs. Doug recognized that the results of his efforts would become evident over time and measurable by the number of accounts he opens. Expecting his first event to begin generating new accounts would have been unrealistic.

Today, Doug is officially courting a number of ultra high net worth individuals with a minimum of 30 million dollars in investible assets.

## Assignment 3:

Let's go back to Worksheet B. Considering the types of events you plan to implement, define your primary and secondary objective for each event.

| Concerns of Tribal Mkt. | Needs of Tribal Mkt. | Potential Topics | Method | Objective |
|---|---|---|---|---|
| Lacking knowledge | Education | Investing 101 | Monthly workshops | 1.<br><br>2. |
| Quality trustworthy money management | Separately Managed Accts | Money Managers | Quarterly featuring money managers | 1.<br><br>2. |
| Confidence in future | Motivation and Inspiration | Health Advice<br><br>Fitness Advice | Annual Health and Wealth symposium | 1.<br><br>2. |

## Creating the Calendar

Okay, now were ready to put it all together. In Chapter 2, we started by building a basic event calendar, posting when you would host a workshop, event, cluster lunch, focus group or seminar. In Chapter 3, we worked on identifying appropriate topics for each style of event. Now, we need to go back to our calendar and clarify not just when the event will take place, but the topic and objective of each event. This will become your working calendar. If used effectively, this calendar can be the blueprint for all of your marketing strategies. Let me give you a brief example of how this calendar can evolve and drive all of your marketing efforts.

1. Assume over the next three months, you are planning a workshop, an event and a seminar. We have determined the topics based on our business model and driven by our tribal market.

| Activity | January | February | March |
|---|---|---|---|
| | | | |
| | **Workshop** Retirement Recovery Plan | **Event** The Power of Annuities | **Focus Lunch** Issues of the new Retirement |

2. The next step is to add additional marketing strategies that lead up to and support the upcoming event. For example, you might add monthly emails to your calendar. With this advanced planning, you can select interesting articles, relevant to your event topic, to enhance your message.

| Activity | January | February | March |
|---|---|---|---|
| | | | |
| **Event** | **Workshop** Retirement Recovery Plan | **Event** The Power of Annuities | **Focus Lunch** Issues of the new Retirement |
| **Email** | **Article:** 10 Steps to rebuilding your retirement | **Article:** How to generate more income | **Article:** What are the hazards going forward |
| **Conference Call** | **Chief economist:** Where do we go from here? | **Lincoln Annuities** The benefits of annuities | **Life Coach:** How to plan for retirement |

Now, what was just an event calendar becomes your complete marketing and communication calendar. Not only does this help you stay focused and organized, but your team/assistant are able to promote your upcoming events in their daily conversations.

> **A well-developed event calendar can allow you to continually market your events.**

It's important that we address the incredible intangible impact of this whole process of planning. When speaking with a client or prospect, you are now able to mention an upcoming event or future article you plan to send. What impression do you think this sends about you, your practice and your level of organization?

By developing and using this calendar, you are better able to present your value, enhance our level of professionalism and increase the level of confidence of both your clients and potential clients. Investors are much more comfortable giving their millions of dollars to those advisors who exude organization and professionalism and are constantly thinking ahead.

Each of these exercises will assist you in creating a master event calendar. This calendar gives you a bird's eye view of all your marketing activities and acts as a working tool to guide all of your marketing efforts. It becomes an incredible marketing tool to clients, prospects, and most importantly, centers of influence (COI's).

## Penetrating that Center of Influence

The marketing aspect of this event calendar is best appreciated when presenting it to a center of influence, otherwise called a COI. A COI is another professional in a different line of business that is also building a practice by looking for new clients. The most common COI's are CPA's and attorneys.

In an introductory presentation with a COI, presenting your calendar of events solidifies in his or her mind not just your commitment to your practice but your professional ability. This is also an important reason to carefully select your venue. At a glance, the title and venue will clearly reflect the quality of events you provide. By providing the COI with the calendar, or even extra copies of the calendar, he or she will have more opportunities to recommend a client, or market your events to clients he feels would be most appropriate for your practice.

> **Your calendar of events is an effective marketing piece with centers of influence.**

This event calendar became a tremendous selling tool for me when trying to differentiate myself from other advisors. After many years of holding events for my clients, I decided to approach the local golf club as a venue. My objective was not only to secure the venue, but to get access to the mailing list of golfers. Pelican Hill, in Newport Beach, was the newest and one of the most sought after courses overlooking the Pacific Ocean. I wanted to capitalize on this new club and intrigue more prospects and clients to participate in my events.

I presented my program to the golf pro. He was very interested and even offered to provide two golf instructors for a free clinic to all of my guests. He specifically commented on the quality of my events, purely based on the event calendars I presented to him. At this point, I suggested he allow the invitations to go to his mailing list as well, with the intent of getting his former clients to revisit the club in hopes of getting them reengaged with his golf program. We scheduled a series of events held at the top of the green including a light lunch and a presentation from a professional manager, followed by an exclusive golf clinic.

I utilized this same concept in approaching a non-profit organization that supported abused children. My calendar of events seemed to tip the scales in my favor. The calendar projects an image of organization, longevity and stability, all qualities that are attractive to joint ventures. Consider your own practice and tribal market; consider opportunities where you too can create an event while leveraging the database of the partnering organization. This process creates a WIN-WIN situation.

> **Your calendar of events sets you apart from the competition.**

Take a moment to list any potential partners that immediately come to mind. Develop this list as you focus on a particular tribal market and new partners will become evident.

Potential Partners:

1. _____

2. _____

3. _____

4. _____

5. _____

## Does It Reflect You?

Your event calendar is a reflection of your business. As you create it, keep in mind how it will appear in the eyes of your clients and prospective clients and the image it projects regarding your business. It is important that you create a format and stay with that format, changing only the event details. Based on your target market and business philosophy, you might even consider adding a quote or saying that reflects you and your practice, kind of like a tag line. Make it fun, personal, and professional.

> **Your event calendar must reflect you, your practice, and your message.**

On the following pages are two samples of calendars, each has a slightly different format and style.

# TITLE OF CALENDAR

## First Quarter Event Calendar

*(Quote)*

| | | |
|---|---|---|
| Jan 15 | Client & Guest | **Alternative Investments:** Understanding how Alternative Investments contribute to your wealth plan. Lunch at the Ritz, Newport Beach 12:00 – 2:00pm |
| Feb 7 | Women clients | **Navigating Transitional Events:** A panel discussion for women experiencing one of life's transitional events, Divorce, Widowhood, becoming a Care Giver. Branch Office – Lunch provided 12:00 – 2:00pm |
| Feb 21 | Clients Only | **2005 and Beyond:** Mitch Wise, Chief Economist, discusses current market environment and what we can expect going forward. Lunch - Four Seasons, Newport Beach 12:00 – 2:00pm |
| Mar 6 | Client & Guests | **Alternative Investments:** Understanding how Alternative   Investments contribute to your wealth plan. Lunch at the Ritz, Newport Beach 6:00 – 7:30pm |
| Mar 18 | Women clients | **Physical and Financial Health:** For women & guests looking to establish a lifetime of Financial Health. Branch Office – Coffee and Bagels 8:00 – 9:30am |

*Seating is limited – RSVP a must*
*(800) 123-4567*

Contact name

**What you learned:**

- Set realistic expectations for your individual events.
- By defining clear objective, you are able to measure your progress.
- Your objectives can be both long term and immediate.
- A well-developed event calendar can allow you to continually market your events.
- Your calendar of events sets you apart from the competition.
- Your event calendar must reflect you, your practice, your message.

# Chapter 5
## Step 4: Selecting the Cast

**What you will learn:**

- **Outside presenters benefit or deficit?**
- **How to insure the presenter supports your objectives**
- **Where to look for presenters**
- **How to get financial support**
- **How to leverage in-house resources**
- **The benefits of building an alliance**
- **Some presenters can be a great referral source**
- **How to solicit interest from COI's**
- **Exceptional Achievers are a great resource**

The purpose of this chapter is to help you recognize that you have many choices when selecting a presenter for your event. Additionally, you will learn how to leverage your presenter to build your audience.

Here is where we separate the men from the boys, the women from the girls the professional speakers from the raconteurs. Let me begin by saying that if done properly, I see no significant benefit or detriment if you are the main speaker or not. Whether you are the presenter or not, you still welcome the guests, deliver a brief introduction, summarize the presentation and close the event. Even with a minor speaking part, you can easily position yourself as an expert and the person who is best suited to invest the participants' money. With that said, now that you have positioned your events through twelve months of the year, it's time to make some decisions.

There are many benefits to bringing in an outside presenter and many factors to consider when making your selection. Having a speaker allows you to spend less time preparing and more time prospecting. An outside presenter is typically experienced in public speaking and can adjust their presentation to meet your objectives. He or she can answer questions and mingle with the guests, encouraging them to work with you. When you have an outside presenter, you can spend more time conversing with your guests, even sitting with them during the presentation.

> **Using an outside presenter can reduce stress, time, energy and resources typically required for an event.**

Once you have decided to enlist the support of an outside presenter, there are a number of factors to consider when making your selection:

- Are you looking for funds to support your event?
- Are you looking for an external presenter who appears more objective?
- Are you looking to build an alliance with an outside professional?

All of these questions play a role in where you begin to look for a presenter and whom you approach. However, your job is not done just because you have a speaker selected and committed your event. Don't assume that just because speakers give presentations all the time that they are good at it.

A speaker who is dry, boring or disorganized will harm your event. Remember, you have an objective in mind; therefore, every part of the presentation should be geared towards achieving that objective. It is your responsibility to make sure that happens. To maintain control over the event, you must coach and guide the presenter to deliver the message that will help you achieve your objectives.

Even though many speakers come with a canned presentation, I think you will find that most are willing to alter their presentation to fit your event. With this in mind, it becomes critical that you are not only crystal clear as to your objective and key points you want covered, but you communicate this information to the presenter with ample time before the event. Most presenters will appreciate your directness and clarity as to what it is you hope to accomplish with the event.

> **When selecting a presenter, you must be prepared to coach them towards your objectives.**

## Clean the Slate

As you begin the process of selecting a presenter, the first thing you need to do is clean the slate. Our tendency is to consider presenters that we have already experienced, limiting our choices. This can cause you to ruin your own event. There is no doubt that these presenters should be part of your selection pool, but limiting your pool denies you the opportunity to think creatively – which is where most of our brilliant ideas originate. It's most important to select a presenter that is right for your tribal market, not necessarily easy and convenient for you.

Think about your event and your goals. If there were no limitations whatsoever, who would you want to speak at your event? This should be your starting point.

If you are able bring in your "ideal" presenter, you should be more than willing to fund the event yourself because you realize the impact he or she will have. Even if you don't have the resources, you will become resourceful and find the funds elsewhere.

The key to this whole selection process is "Think Big." Don't limit your thoughts. Work from your vision and you will be amazed what you can create. For example, you may know a professional athlete, president of a university, CEO of a major company or a local company. An attorney, CPA or life coach can all be appropriate presenters, depending on your topic and focus. Do some brainstorming and start building your list.

> **When selecting your presenter THINK BIG and be creative.**

Once you have created a list of desirable presenters, who all compliment and support the message you are trying to project, begin considering other factors. These other factors help you identify which presenter brings the greatest additional value to the event, your business, and future possibilities.

## Show Me the Money

Finding resources to fund your event is the first thing many FA's consider when selecting a presenter. But if funding becomes your primary concern, it can derail all of your efforts. You are already putting a tremendous amount of time, energy, and resources into sponsoring an event that can help to grow your business. Don't sacrifice the quality. There are a number of ways to get financial support for your events. The most common are wholesalers who may benefit from sales from your event. Some of the more common sources of funding are:

- Mutual funds wholesalers
- Annuity reps
- Insurance reps
- Professional money managers

> **Product wholesalers can be a great resource for your events.**

As our industry evolves, so to do the laws governing the benefits and perks available through product wholesalers. Be mindful of the rules and think creatively in order to get the support you need and the funding you desire.

Another way to defer some of the expenses associated with events is through cost sharing. You can use cost sharing in several ways. Holding an event with other financial advisors allows you to host (what appears to be) a larger event, yet you are only responsible for your own guests.

Working with professionals outside of the industry is a very lucrative way of cost sharing, especially when you are able to send invites to their database as well. In most situations, when you are willing to commit some of your own funds to the event, other companies and reps will be more considerate of your request. In addition, don't hesitate to consider a combination of presenters. This reduces the financial commitment for each speaker. Be sure however, you have a clear agenda and that the two presenters are willing to work with each other and with the overall objective of supporting you and your business.

> **Share the cost of your event with outside presenters and other financial advisors.**

During my years in production, I sponsored a luncheon every month at the Ritz in Newport Beach, featuring two money managers with complimentary styles. For example, I might have an international manager with a domestic manager, or a small cap manager with a bond manager. I found that both presenters not only positioned me as the expert, but supported each other and created a collaborative environment. Each presenter paid just one third of the cost.

Considering your tribal market and their core issues and concerns, start a list of wholesalers that you feel would be appropriate partners in your event program.

## Appropriate Wholesalers:

1. _____

2. _____

3. _____

4. _____

5. _____

**Internal Presenters:** Certainly, using your internal resources can be a source of financial support, but more importantly, their value lies primarily in their desire to support your efforts. In addition, by bringing in a top-ranking representative from your own firm, the perception is that your firm values you. This can elevate your status in the minds of your clients and prospects.

However, even with internal presenters, don't assume they are effective at articulating their message. Coaching and guidance continue to be critical components with every presenter, regardless of the source. Make sure that each presenter has a clear understanding of your tribal market and their needs, as well as the objective of the event.

Internal presenters do not have to be limited to product areas, consider the following:

- Analyst
- Economists
- Corporate Managers
- Directors
- Portfolio Managers
- Strategists
- Branch Managers
- Product Specialists: Estate Planning, Lending, Retirement Planning, Private Banking Executives

> **Internal presenters can be very supportive of your events.**

**Potential Internal Presenters:** As you consider your tribal market, list any internal presenters that fit your needs.

1. _____

2. _____

3. _____

4. _____

5. _____

## Alliances with External Professionals

Building alliances with professionals outside of the financial services industry can add tremendous value to your presentation. They appear more objective, can give you additional exposure to their client base (remember the golf pro), and can eventually become a great source of referrals. External presenters can come from all walks of life, so your primary considerations should be their value to your event, their public speaking skills, and their ability to support your message.

> **External presenters can be a source of referrals.**

Many brilliant individuals are excellent at what they do yet can bore an audience to sleep. If this is the case, their value to your event goes into the negative zone since you can lose credibility in the minds of your audience. So, how do we prevent this from happening? I highly recommend you do your research before selecting an outside presenter. Ask for speaking referrals, sit in on one of their upcoming presentations, and ask them for the three key points to their presentation. This will help you determine whether they have a clear message or whether they will be all over the board, confusing the audience to delirium.

If you can find an external presenter that compliments your message, has proven presentation skills, is able to support your objective, and is willing to add some of their clients to the event, you have truly reached nirvana. Sound unlikely? Think again. Attorneys, CPA's, and business consultants are all looking to build their business. Recognizing you have similar tribal markets and complimentary styles of business can create a win–win for both of you. These individuals now become your business partners. Remember, business partners are those who work in a field that related to or complementing your work as a financial professional. For example:

- CPA's
- Divorce attorneys
- Civil attorneys
- Estate attorneys
- Liability attorneys
- Patent attorneys
- Lenders
- Real estate agents
- Business consultants
- Business insurers

As long as you focus on one particular tribal market, you will uncover additional professionals, specific to your tribe that you might not have otherwise identified.

> **Building alliances with outside professionals can create a referral stream for life.**

Potential Business Partners: Make a list of potential external presenters to consider and evaluate.

## CPA's

_____

_____

_____

## Attorneys

_____

_____

_____

## Other categories

_____

_____

_____

## Let's take it a step further

There are a number of things to consider when developing an alliance with another professional.

- Are they accepting new clients?
- Do they already have an exclusive relationship with another financial professional?
- What is their area of expertise?
- What is their typical client profile?
- Do they have an existing client base?
- Are they looking to grow their practice?
- Are they willing to joint market the event?
- Do they maintain a list of dormant clients?
- Where and how do they advertise their practice?

Janice Goldman, a financial consultant in Illinois, targets professional women. To better leverage her efforts, Janice developed an alliance with a female attorney also specializing in working with women. Together, they sponsor many events, inviting both their clients, creating a club-like atmosphere where women felt comfortable. Janice and the attorney have become valuable referral sources for each other's business.

Angela Keaveny, financial advisor, developed a relationship with an executive coach. Together they address the needs and issues of executives in their mutual target market.

Julia Duncan, in San Diego, California, targeted business owners, specifically those looking to sell their business. Julia held a series of events collaborating with business attorneys and business consultants, creating a network to support this type of client.

No matter whom you collaborate with for your events, be sure to spend ample time clarifying the objective and refining your three key points. And, don't forget to practice your presentations together before presenting in front of your clients and prospects.

## Do You Know an Exceptional Achiever?

There are other types of external presenters that don't add financial support or alliance value, but are highly attractive to your target audience. These exceptional achievers inspire interest purely by their accomplishments, and many times have little or no relationship to the financial world. I'm sure you know someone who is exceptional in his or her field. Here are just a few to consider:

- Plastic surgeons
- Professional snow boarders
- Professional rainmakers
- Medical specialists
- Mountain climbers
- Military officers
- Fashion consultants
- Wine connoisseurs
- Famous artists
- Well-known musicians
- Non-profits
- Nutritionists
- Psychologists

Although these achievers have no direct relationship to the financial industry, they can attract clients and prospects to your event.

In many cases, these types of presenters great for client appreciation events. Client appreciation events do NOT necessarily have to be for "clients" only. A presenter who generates interest is a great opportunity to encourage your clients to bring a friend or associate.

So, although the objective of a client appreciation event is to show how much you value your client and their business, a secondary objective could be to generate more introductions. In addition, this achiever sets you apart from the competition by adding value in ways other than stocks and bonds. It is your job to apply some principle, process, or activity from the presenter's message and tie it to a concept or activity related to the financial services industry.

> **Exceptional achievers create greater interest in your event and set you apart from other financial advisors.**

Keith Schuss, a financial consultant in Ohio, targets local attorneys in his community. Four times a year, Keith has a professional rainmaker come to his monthly event. This professional does not share his client base with Keith, but draws such a large crowd and is such a big attraction that Keith always generates a number of new prospects. In addition, Keith elevates his reputation and image in the community of attorneys while building a tremendous amount of good will.

The Kelly Group, a financial consultant team out of New Jersey, recently brought in a plastic surgeon and a nutritionist for two women's events. The events generated tremendous interest; they had 100% attendance with 50% of the participants being new prospects.

Jeremy and Roger Vlach, financial advisors in Oregon, consider themselves "Active Wealth Managers." Most of their clients are very active individuals and families, who prefer to spend their time enjoying the outdoors and leaving the financial aspects of their lives to the Vlachs. The Vlachs sponsored a client appreciation event featuring a professional snow boarder, and encouraged their clients to bring guests.

You set yourself apart when you provide events featuring presenters that are unrelated to the financial services industry, purely by addressing the non-financial needs of your client. By focusing on your tribal market, you zero in on what really adds value. This type of value instills client loyalty, creates a community atmosphere, and allows both you and your clients to enjoy a different aspect to your relationship.

## Exceptional Achievers to Consider:

1. _____

2. _____

3. _____

**What you learned:**
- Using an outside presenter can reduce stress, time, energy and resources typically required for an event.
- When selecting a presenter, be prepared to coach them towards your objectives.
- When selecting your presenter, THINK BIG and be creative.
- Product wholesalers can be a great resource for your events.
- Share the cost of your event with outside presenters and other financial advisors.
- Internal presenters can be very supportive of your events.
- External presenters can be a source of referrals.
- Building alliances with outside professionals can create a referral stream for life.
- Exceptional achievers create greater interest in your event and set you apart from other financial advisors.

# Chapter 6

## Step 5: A Venue that Adds Value

**What you will learn:**

- **What to look for in a venue**
- **The three criteria in your selection process**
- **How to create a comfortable environment**
- **The impact of dessert on your success**

The purpose of this chapter is to emphasize the importance of your venue, how to identify a venue that will add value to your event and enhance your ability to achieve your goals.

A proper venue can add tremendous value to your event, can attract a better audience, and deter those looking for a "free meal." It can elevate your status in the minds of your clients while helping to make the event run smoothly. All of this increases your ability to have a successful event. So, what determines the "proper" venue? You must consider the following three key criteria:

1. The venue must set a tone that reflects the level of professionalism in your business.
2. The venue must have the proper space to ensure privacy and enhance the environment you are trying to create.
3. The venue must have the proper facilities and accommodations, and the staff must be well versed in managing events

Each criterion becomes a critical component to the success of your event. When you have found a venue that meets all three of the criteria, you have increased your chances of achieving your objectives.

> **The appropriate venue must reflect you and your practice, have the proper facilities and accommodations and the right space conducive to private conversation.**

To determine if a venue is a reflection of you and your practice, you must start by looking at your tribal market. What interests and meets the needs of your tribal market will be the biggest factor in choosing a venue. Is the venue appealing to your audience? Does it set the tone for the quality of events and the level of clients you are seeking to attract?

Different venues appeal to different tribal markets. An event at The Ritz or the Four Seasons may be completely unappealing to individuals in a more rural or agricultural setting, whereas the local library may hold little attraction to a highly sophisticated audience.

Select a venue that would be appealing to the audience regardless of the topic or style of event. If in doubt, make a few calls and ask your favorite clients, clients that represent your tribal market, about their three favorite restaurants. This will give you an idea of where you should be looking.

> **The selection process starts with what is appealing to your tribal market. If in doubt, just ask them.**

An associate of mine used to hold his events at Polly's Pies, a higher-end coffee shop, where he would reserve a private room set for thirty guests. It was important that he overbook the event because he always had a large percentage of no shows and many of the participants seemed to have little interest in the topic and would only attend for the food. He ended up paying for many extra meals just to get a few good accounts.

This was a very common process during the days when we were cold calling with products. It was also not uncommon to get an appointment to open an account immediately following the event. Many investors during this time had multiple accounts, depending on the "product" of the day.

Bill Good created a whole program around these volume types of events. They were held in low cost restaurants or banquet rooms. The advisor would call just a few days before the event to ask the participant if they prefer the chicken or beef dish. This was a subtle way of reaffirming the commitment of the participant and helping to reduce the No-Show list. Although these events and systems were effective in their day, our industry has evolved and these "turn 'em and burn 'em" events lost their appeal.

In the mid 90's things were different. I held many of my events at The Four Seasons or the Ritz Restaurant in Newport Beach, California, and limited the list to fifteen guests, a fact I noted on the invitation. I rarely had less than a 95% turnout and many times had more than 100% show up, forcing me to shuffle tables at the last minute (this is a good problem to have and sends a positive message to the other participants). Rarely did I have guests coming just for the food. People are more apt to take advantage of a $5.00 breakfast in a room of thirty people than a $30.00 lunch with fifteen or less.

Needless to say, I attracted high-quality individuals and prospects who were interested in the topic. Unless I had a compelling reason to change my venue, I stuck with what worked. No one ever tired of lunching at these upscale restaurants. In addition, because of the continuity and frequency of my events, I became very comfortable with the wait staff and they with me. This made the whole process easier, with less stress and increased the level of professionalism. If you find something that works, stick with it. When you select a venue that is not appropriate for your market, you run a high risk of attracting few or no participants or paying for a lot of free lunches.

> **If you want to attract high-end clients, find a high-end venue that works and stick with it.**

Next, you want to make sure that the venue has the right space, conducive to privacy and enhancing the environment you are trying to create. You must visit the venue and scout it out.

Mostly likely, you will want to repeat your events at the same venue, so make sure it can accommodate large number attendee events and smaller group events. Remember, it's better if the room is too small than too big.

For instance, if you are planning on fifteen to twenty participants, have two rounds with eight guests at a table. Better that the guests are rubbing shoulders than too widely spaced out. The tighter the setting, the more conversation will ensue. The more spread out the room, the less energy, and less likely there will be small talk among attendees. We all have a tendency to give people plenty of personal space, not a good approach when hosting events.

The flooring can have an impact as well. Carpeting helps to mute sound and creates a warmer environment. Regardless of how well you think you can project, ALWAYS defer to a microphone and be sure the facilities can accommodate your needs. No one wants to be at an event where they can't hear the speaker. In addition, many of our high net worth clients may be in their later years, making the volume even more important. Check the air temperature. How it is controlled? Don't forget about the elevator music that can often be a distraction to your event.

You must visit the room personally. If you intend to have a podium, be sure that everyone can see you. Be sure that no one ends up sitting behind a pillar bobbing back and forth in order to maintain contact with you.

> **It's better to have a room too small than a room too big.**

Be sure there is room for a reception table and that the facilities can supply audiovisual equipment. Be careful here. Using the venue's equipment can incur substantial costs. Clarify this in advance. An important criterion is the sound system. It's important that there is a microphone and even better, lavalieres (clip-on mikes). If you will be using PowerPoint or projectors, be sure they have the appropriate set up, as well as a screen that can be seen by everyone in the room. Ensure any mood music can be turned off and that you are familiar with the lighting.

Finally, it's important that the staff is able to accommodate your needs and enhance the overall atmosphere. Find out who will be in charge the day of your event. Introduce yourself and take the time to share the agenda. Get any parking issues clarified and make sure that guests will be directed to the appropriate room – either by signage or by staff. Find out the timing of any meals, so that everything is set to run smoothly.

> **Get to know the wait staff.**

Venues can range from,

- Restaurants
- Libraries
- Golf courses
- Museums

- Jewelry stores
- Department stores
- Theatres
- Wine cellars
- Your home

**Venues:** List five venues to consider for future events.

1. _____

2. _____

3. _____

4. _____

5. _____

# The Results are in the Dessert

Finally, it's important that you select an appropriate menu. Again, before we can begin to select the food, it is important to consider the needs and lifestyle of your tribal market. What is most important is that you provide ample food and quality service with the least amount of commotion or activity.

A buffet is an event killer in my book. With a buffet, you lose control of the timing of the event and the people are getting up and down during your presentation. I prefer a preset meal with dessert and coffee to follow. Most quality restaurants have a banquet menu. Always pre-select the meal.

Although you can go with three-courses (salad, main course, dessert), during a business lunch, I prefer a main plate that combines the main course and vegetables with pre-set desserts. This prevents excessive serving, clanging noises, and hubbub associated with serving a meal. But again, it all depends on your target market, how well the individuals know each other, how much time you have allotted, and the purpose of the event.

I would be more inclined to allow multiple courses for appreciation events as well as dinner events. I would also discourage you from giving the guest any choices to select during the event. If you do prefer to give them a choice of entrees, use it as a way of solidifying their commitment to attending the event beforehand.

> **Keep it simple and tasteful.**

It is important that you pay particular attention to the timing of the meal and the event. Let me give you an idea of how I timed my events.

As clients come to our private room, I greet them and introduce my assistant. Since we have assigned seats, I escort my clients to my table and their seats. If they are the first to arrive, I casually chat with them or share why I was looking forward to this event. Hopefully, I gain enough information so that when the next guests arrive I can share my new knowledge of the guests, which automatically causes the participants to strike up conversation. For example, as I walk Mr. and Mrs. Smith to the table, I learn that they do volunteer work at the local museum.

Once they are seated and I see additional guests have arrived, I excuse myself and go to greet the new guests. While walking them to the table, I learn that Mr. and Mrs. Jones live in Harbor View Hills, very close to the museum. When we reach the table, I make sure to introduce the couples and share the little bit of information I learned about each one. This tends to get the couples warming up with conversation.

> **Introduce your guests to each other to help create a more comfortable atmosphere.**

Once all my clients are seated, I don't stand around twiddling my thumbs, like many advisors do, but I take my seat with my guests. I mention the presentation we are about to hear and ask my guests questions to learn their level of sophistication and understanding. Even though I give the introduction to the presentation, I stay with my guests until I am needed. When the room is

80-90% full, I signal to the maître d to start serving the main course (chicken with vegetables and small salad). Once I see that everyone has a plate in front of them, I get up and open up the event.

During the presentation (assuming I am not the speaker), I sit at the table with my guests and I make sure to take notes. These notes become valuable at the end of the event. Sometimes, I share them during the Q&A session with the presenter, but more times than not, after closing out the event, I sit back down with my guests and use those notes as topics for discussion. Because I made sure the desserts were unusual, most guests stay for dessert and coffee. My table and guests are inevitably the last to leave.

> **Be sure to sit with your guests in order to increase communication and the level of intimacy.**

When I first started hosting my events as a financial advisor, I would share my events with other financial advisors in my branch, thereby increasing the number of participants in the room. I made sure to limit my guests to one table only – anywhere from eight to twelve at a table.

After a number of successful events, one of the participating FA's asked me what I talk about at my table. Wondering what prompted the question, I asked him "Why do you ask?" Much to my delight, he said "As soon as the event is over, all my guests get up and leave, but all of your guests are still sitting at your table for at least thirty minutes after the event, all engaged in conversation and enjoying their coffee and dessert." I told the FA it was all in the dessert.

> **A decadent dessert keeps your guests to the end of the event.**

As you visit different venues, consider the overall atmosphere. What is the message it sends your clients and prospects? Does it reflect the image that you want to project and is it attractive to the kind of clients you are looking for? Will the facilities create any challenges or will they enhance the overall experience of your guests? Did the staff seem cooperative, engaged with a positive attitude? Most important, have your decisions been driven by the interest of your tribal market?

When planning my first large seminar, I first considered my tribal market. I had two lists I was working with – a local church roster and a volunteer roster from the local botanical gardens. Considering the women on these lists, I decided to hold a "Socially Aware Investing" event at the restaurant on the grounds of the botanical gardens. The event site was completely appropriate and drew a great crowd. The facilities were set up in advance allowing for a seamless event, and I was able to focus on my presentation and converse with my guests."

As long as you allow your tribal market to drive your decisions, you will have a much greater success rate.

> **To ensure success listen to your tribal market.**

Venue Checklist:
- Is it attractive to my target market?
- Can they accommodate different size events?
- Do they have private rooms?
- Do they provide audiovisual equipment?
  - Mike
  - Lavaliere
  - Projector
  - Extension cord
- Do they provide signage?
- Do they have a podium?
- Do they have a reception table?
- Do they provide free parking?
- Who is the person in charge?
- Is their menu appealing?

**What you learned:**

- The appropriate venue must reflect you and your practice, have the proper facilities and accommodations and the proper space, conducive to private conversation.
- The selection process starts with what is appealing to your tribal market. If in doubt just ask them.
- If you want to attract high-end clients, find a high-end venue that works and stick with it.
- It's better to have a room too small than a room too big.
- Get to know the wait staff.
- Keep it simple and tasteful.
- Introduce your guests to each other to help create a more comfortable atmosphere.
- Be sure to sit with your guests to increase communication and level of intimacy.
- A decedent dessert keeps your guests to the end of the event.
- To ensure success, listen to your tribal market.

# Chapter 7
## Step 6: Marketing the Plan

**What you will learn:**

- **How to effectively market your event**
- **What type of invitation works best**
- **How to get your invitation opened**
- **How to utilize email for your events**
- **How to utilize your event calendar**

In this chapter, we focus on how to market your events, when to use mailed invites or email, the factors that get your invite opened and how your event calendar can support and enhance your event marketing.

You've developed the foundation for your multi-tiered seminar program and you know the frequency of events, the topics that appeal to your market, and the venues and potential speakers. Now, it's time to leverage this foundation and begin your strategic marketing.

There are three basic ways to market your events. The first and most common is via an invitation – whether wedding style, flyer, or save-the-date -- using the US post office.

The second is via email. This cost effective method can be used in lieu of physical invites or to support and compliment the actual invite.

The final method is utilizing your calendar of events. The calendar of events increases your ability to leverage these events, is less expensive and adds more long-term marketing benefits than a single invitation.

There are advantages to all three methods and your decision does not have to be limited to just one. In my own practice, I often used all three methods for a single event. The different styles of events, circumstances, and tribal markets will help you determine the most effective method for generating participation and interest in your events.

## Invitations

There are many varieties of invitations, as well as choices of how to create and present them. You can hand deliver, invite by phone, send invitations via e-mail, or go the traditional route and use the US mail. Remember, you are using three different types of events, so hand delivery would not be feasible for a seminar but is appropriate for an exclusive event of less than fifteen guests. I've found that a combination of all three invitation methods increases your response rate.

Before you determine the method of delivery, you have to create the invitation. Too many invitations give multiple bullet points explaining what will be addressed at the event; others look like a business letter stating the facts with little or no creativity.

If you want your invitation to get noticed…

## Keep it simple

Less is more. The invitation should be designed to intrigue and attract, not to educate or sell. Focus on the issue at hand and show the recipient you have the solution. Don't drown them in information. Send too much information and recipients will disqualify themselves from attending.

> **An invitation should intrigue the recipient NOT educate.**

> ## *"Bridging the Longevity Gap"*
> *STRATEGIES AND VEHICLES TO HELP MAINTAIN YOUR INCOME DURING RETIREMENT*

## Be creative

As financial advisors, creativity may not be your strong suit. Not to worry, consider tapping into friends, family members, or a graphic designer to help create an invitation that reflects your style and can be used over and over again. Remember, when you are developing an event program, the more consistent your message the better. This also pertains to the format of the invitation. If you are constantly changing the design, it tends to be a bit confusing for the recipients.

By staying with a defined format and just changing the title and content, you make it easy for the recipient to absorb the information while also peaking their interest. If you lack those creative genes, consider hiring a good designer to create a professional template that reflects your style. Once they have designed the template, you can use that same format for all of your marketing materials. Have fun with fonts, size and colors; the more unique the more it will get noticed.

> **Design a standard template to use for all of your invitations.**

As you create the invite, you want to give enough information to catch the invitee's interest but not so much as to disqualify themselves. By listing all of the topics and points of interest, you may be shooting yourself in the foot.

In addition, you want to create a sense of urgency or create the need to respond ASAP. Most people procrastinate making decisions. As they procrastinate, they lose interest and often forget about your event. By creating the sense of urgency, you push them to make a commitment early on, allowing you the opportunity to follow up and enhance their commitment. Here are a few examples of how to heighten the response rate:

Space is limited
RSVP a must
Call to find out if you qualify/if this is appropriate for you
Limited opportunity

> **Creating a sense of urgency heightens the commitment.**

Make sure your invitation is opened and read. This is the most important aspect of the process. It really doesn't matter what the invitation says or looks like, if no one ever sees it. If it isn't opened, everything you have done has been for naught. So often, financial advisors spend lots of time, money and resources planning for the event, and then scrimp on the mailing process to save a few dollars. Yet if the invite ends up in the trash can, it really doesn't matter what you spent on what. It's all a loss.

The goal is to make the invitation stand out, and especially stand apart from all the junk mail. There are a number of things you can do that will help ensure the envelope gets opened.

The size of the invitation can make the difference between a boring business letter and a fun educational event. Although invitations and envelopes with a unique size may cost a little more, the impact can justify the cost.

Another way to create interest in your invitation, which may be less costly than wedding style invites, is using different colored paper with matching envelopes. With colored paper, you can use letter size paper and envelopes and still generate the interest that gets the invite opened.

The font of your invite can play a role in creating interest. Fonts can make an event look casual, formal, fun, or serious. Even the size of the font can help the process. How it's spaced can have a positive or negative impact. It's best to pick one font and perhaps two sizes, a standard size and a large size for emphasis. Don't make the invite too busy by incorporating multiple font styles and sizes. This can detract from your message, causing the recipient to focus more on the invitation style than the message.

If you are not sure what looks good, share it with a few friends or family members. Ask for their initial reaction to the invite. Don't coach them though. Don't ask them how it looks or do they like the look. Just present the invite and ask for their initial thoughts. They won't know if you are asking about the style or the content. See what they say.

> **The size, font and color of the invitation can enhance the chances of getting it opened.**

Regardless of what style envelopes you use, hand writing the addresses gives the invitation a more personal touch. And no, handwritten with invisible labels are nice but still do not have the same impact as your everyday handwriting. I found I could easily address about 100 invitations while watching TV for an hour at night. If you are like my husband, who has the handwriting of a doctor, you can pay a student with good handwriting to address your envelopes. A hand-written envelope is one of the most effective methods of getting the recipient to open the invitation. Never use pre-printed labels.

> **Handwritten envelope combined with a postage stamp ensures your invitation gets opened.**

If you go to all the effort to handwrite the envelope, then seriously consider using a real stamp for postage. Unique size, combined with handwritten envelopes and real postage is the secret to making sure all your intended guests open their invitations. Depending on the number of invitations you send, at 42 cents it won't cost that much and the benefits will be so worth it.

I've even heard it said that putting the stamp on a little crooked adds to the personal look and increases the chances of it getting opened. There is no doubt that a postage stamp is received more enthusiastically than a bulk mail, machine-printed stamp.

> **A crooked postage stamp makes the envelope more personal.**

Another creative way to get your invitation opened is with lumpy mail. With lumpy mail, you can even use labels or business size invites, it's the lumpiness that entices the recipient to open it. Lumpy mail is when you put something in the envelope that either shakes, makes noise or just creates a lump to the envelope. Rarely will people throw lumpy mail away without opening it.

Your firm may have some small rulers or letter openers that can easily fit into the envelope. My favorite is chocolate coins. This creates the lumpiness while also emphasizing your role in finance. Some advisors to put a pack of seeds for the money plant in the envelopes.

Next time you go to a toy store, look around at things that are inexpensive, small enough to stuff into an envelope and also have some connection with your role as a financial advisor. Have fun with this, the more fun you have the more effective you will be.

> **Lumpy mail should be fun and creative and can be used with business style envelopes.**

## Email Invitations

Email can be a very effective method for marketing your events. It costs nothing and takes very little time.

If you are emailing to new prospects who have never heard of you, you may be better off sending a physical invitation. But, if your event program has been developed and established, email will generate better results. Financial advisors who have developed a reputation for hosting regular events tend to use email as their method for distributing invitations. Their clients have come to expect invites via their in-box, therefore this becomes one of the most effective and efficient methods of marketing their events. Again, I want to emphasize that these advisors have created and established a consistent event program.

For those initiating events for the first time, I do not recommend depending on email invitations alone. Actually, if you are rolling out your events for the first time, I highly recommend that you invest in some mailed invites and make sure they get opened. A wedding style invitation creates a greater stir than an invitation received via email. Email can sometimes diminish the importance of the event, making it less exclusive and appealing.

A combination of mail and email can be a highly effective process, even with brand new prospects. Consider using email for a, "Save the Date," announcement. Follow that by sending a physical invite through the US mail then follow that with a, "Last chance to RSVP," email. For new prospects, think of email as a way of complimenting and supporting your invites. In addition, with your own email link provided, it is easier for a recipient to RSVP than to pick up the phone to make a call.

> **Using email to support and enhance your physical invitation can increase your response rate.**

If you plan to use email as your invitation method, you still want to pay attention to the style and how it is received. Attachments add an extra step. Unless you can entice the recipient to want to open the attachment, it's always best if the actual email text is the invite. Some advisors create the invite on PowerPoint and then paste the PowerPoint slide into their email. This gives a bit more formal, boxed look, which is dramatically different from a regular, typed email.

Once you have come up with an email template, all you have to do is change the text each time you send it. Again, there may be a minor investment up front to get things started but from there on it becomes quite automated.

> **Attachments to an email add an extra step.**

In most cases, I recommend a physical invitation followed by an email reminder until your event program has developed some traction. Even then, I might mail physical invites to any new additions to my prospecting pipeline until they have attended at least one event. Once they have seen me in person and heard me live, only then would I switch over and start sending email invitations.

## Leveraging the Calendar

The third method of promoting your events is with your calendar of events. The event calendar allows you to cluster a group of events together and combine them in a single marketing piece. By effectively using this calendar, the value of your seminar program goes well beyond the individual events.

This is where your calendar of events becomes a valuable marketing tool as well as saves you time, money, and resources. Think of the calendar as a separate tool all together. Although it does help to promote your events, its impact goes well beyond the actual invite. There are very few financial advisors who know what they will be doing next month, much less in the next three months. When your clients and prospects receive your calendar of events, your image and level of professionalism instantly elevates to a much higher level.

Additionally, if you create your calendar on harder stock paper or make it colorful, there is a better chance that it will go up on the refrigerator or on the office bulletin board as a reminder. Again, another opportunity to reach new people.

I would send my calendar of events at the beginning of every quarter to all prospects and clients. After someone has attended your event and seen you in person, then you can start emailing the invitations while continuing to send the calendar of events on a quarterly basis. Because they have now met you, you no longer need to send a physical invite. However, even with a well-established event program, I recommend using individual invitations for specialty events, mailed to clients, warm prospects (those that know you) and cold prospect alike.

This calendar of events can be used in multiple ways. It is best leveraged by mailing it to every client, prospect, friend, and COI that has either met you or would welcome something from you. I would also consider emailing and posting your calendar on your website. In today's environment, with the click of a button your clients can forward your calendar to multiple friends and colleagues.

This calendar, sent in both physical form as well as electronically, may be the only way you market your events with clients and familiar prospects. Or, depending on the event, you may want to send the calendar followed by an individual invitation. We don't want to bombard our clients and prospects with too much mail. We do want to be sure to reinforce important events to increase chances of getting a positive response. Mailing or emailing your calendar on a quarterly basis, adds to your level of professionalism, consistency and dependability in the mind of the client and prospect.

> **Your event calendar can be emailed, mailed or posted to your website.**

Although individual invites and calendars of events are the main method of marketing your events, there are other activities you can integrate into your plan that help support and promote a more bountiful response.

**A save-the-date announcement** can be mailed or e-mailed in advance of the invitation. This increases the perception of importance of your event and gives recipients advance notice. Use this selectively; if overused it negates the impact. Again, keep the save-the-date vague and intriguing.

**A last chance reminder** can be mailed or emailed sometime between when the invitation is received by the recipient and the event date itself. The purpose is to remind your clients and prospects, while also creating a sense of urgency or demand. By stating that the event is filling up with only a few spots remaining, you increase the attractiveness of the event in the minds of the recipient.

Remember, you don't want to use both of the above methods at once nor repeatedly. Be selective. Mix it up a bit. Use a save-the-date if you already sent the calendar. With a formal invite, you may want to send the reminder. The key is to emphasize and create momentum with your event, without turning them off to receiving information from you.

> **Effective methods to support your event and reinforce the invitation are, "Save the Date," and, "Last Chance," reminders.**

Here's how a timeline might work:

| Jan 1 | Quarterly calendar of events sent to all clients, familiar prospects, and COI's |
|---|---|
| Jan 15 | Save-the-date e-mail or US mail |
| Jan 30 | Invitation mailed via US Post Office |
| Feb 2 | Begin calling on each invitation to encourage RSVP |
| Feb 7 | Event reminder – e-mailed to all clients encouraging they bring a guest |
| Feb 15 | The Event |

## Wait, we're not done yet

Don't assume that the pieces you created around this event will express the true value of the event to the recipient. Only YOU can do that. For this reason, it's important to call each of the recipients to reinforce your excitement for the upcoming event and the impact it will have on their financial future.

Over the years, we have lost one of the most important factors in hosting events. An invitation gives you a more welcome reason for calling a perfect stranger and initiating conversation. It's the conversation part we forgot. For years, I have heard financial advisors calling on their events with little enthusiasm, creating little or no interest. The focus of their call was typically:

"Did you receive the invitation we sent you this week?"

Now really, how is this question going to help you? I prefer to assume they received the invite and immediately launch into the excitement of the event. Next, the typical advisor asks, "Will you be able to attend the event?" soliciting a yes/no answer. They do little to no probing or profiling the prospect. Don't forget, the real value of these events is to generate conversation. By engaging in conversation, you have the ability to uncover whether this event or perhaps one of your other events would be of interest to the recipient. Because you have planned ahead, you know what your events will be about in the next months. You now have the opportunity to generate further interest in the participant. The bottom line is, you must get on the phone.

> **To ensure a good turnout for your event, YOU MUST GET ON THE PHONE.**

When making your call, the purpose is two-fold. You want to encourage the recipient to attend the event, but you also want to initiate or further develop the relationship by engaging in conversation. A typical call sounds something like this:

*"Hello Mr. Smith, Fred Howard from ABC Financial. I'm calling to follow up on an invitation we sent you. Did you receive it? Will you be able to make this event?" I'm sorry to hear that, perhaps you will be able to make our next event. Have a good day."*

That was basically a wasted phone call. Here's a better way to engage the prospect in conversation:

*"Mr. Smith, Evan Enthusiast from Elementary Planning. I'm really excited about our upcoming event. We sent you an invitation, but I wanted to personally invite you because I think you would really enjoy the topic of conversation. Paul Presenter from ABC Management is a fabulous presenter; and considering what's going on in the markets today, he should be able to give us some timely advice. In fact, what do you consider the greatest challenges in the markets today?" Or, "How have these markets impacted your financial future? The event is set for Wed. Jan 15th, and we have a wonderful lunch planned as well. Can I reserve a place for you? Great! Why don't I pencil in a guest for you? That way, you can invite a friend or associate who might also find this topic of value."*

Now let's assume they can't make the event. You may want to consider an approach something like this:

*"The event is set for Wed. Jan 15th, and we have a wonderful lunch planned as well. Can I reserve a place for you? No? I'm sorry to hear that. Tell me, if you were able to attend this event, what would you hope to learn from Paul?" Or, "No? I'm sorry to hear that. We have two more events on the upcoming calendar, (state the title of the events) which of these would be of the most interest to you? Why?"*

> **Use the invite call to create conversation and start the profiling process.**

Remember, the more you can share how this event applies to the recipient's specific situation, the more you increase their desire to attend the event. If they are unable to attend, it at least opens the door to further conversations.

This is an important concept. A seminar is just a way of opening up conversation with the participant. In many cases, you may or may not want the person to actually attend the event and this call is a way to qualify the individual. A good way to qualify is to ask:

*"Mr. Evans, this particular event is best suited for those that have more than$500,000 of invest-able assets. Would this be an appropriate event for you at this time?"*

Remember, our ultimate goal is to get these individuals to become your clients; the seminar is just one way to initiate and develop a good relationship with the prospect.

**What you learned:**

- An invitation should intrigue the recipient NOT educate.
- Design a standard template to use for all of your invitations.
- Creating a sense of urgency heightens the commitment
- The size, font and color of the invitation can enhance the chances of getting it opened.
- Handwritten envelopes, combined with a postage stamp ensure your invitation gets opened.
- A crooked postage stamp makes the envelope more personal.
- Lumpy mail should be fun and creative and can be used with business style envelopes.
- Using email to support and enhance your physical invitation can increase your response rate.
- Attachments to an email add an extra step.
- Your event calendar can be a valuable marketing tool.
- Your event calendar can be emailed, mailed or posted to your website.
- Effective methods to support your event and reinforce the invitation are, "Save the Date," and "Last Chance," reminders.
- To ensure a good turnout for your event, YOU MUST GET ON THE PHONE.
- Use the invite call to create conversation and start the profiling process.

# Chapter 8

## Step 7: Elevating the Commitment

**You will learn:**

- **How to you ensure 100% turn out to your events**
- **What pre-work is and how it helps my event**
- **The multiple benefits of confirmation calls**

The purpose of this chapter is to show you methods that will increase the opportunity to achieve 100% turnout for your events. You will also learn the value of using pre-work and how to elevate the interest in your event.

The first and most important objective in hosting an event is to get enough people to RSVP to fill the room. What a relief it is when you reach your goal of participants. What a letdown when half of the guests don't show. When you have a high no-show ratio, odds are you didn't follow my program. If you had, you would have done one or both of the following.

To ensure your guests commitment, you called the day before the event to confirm their attendance, at which point you reignited their original desire to attend. Secondly, you were very proactive and sent the planned participants pre-work.

Pre-work sets you apart from the competition and increases your guests' commitment and desire to attend the upcoming event. By providing those that RSVP'd some type of pre-work related to the topic, you further motivate their attendance, and create a more receptive environment before the event even begins.

> **Both pre-work and confirmation calls increases the chances of achieving 100% attendance at your event.**

So, what do I mean by pre-work? Pre-work is something to complete before the event, engaging the soon to be guest into the topic or process you plan to present. Pre-work helps to get your guests into the right frame of mind, strengthening their commitment and desire to show up at your event.

Pre-work can take many different forms. You could send a brochure or article that applies to the topic, highlighting just a piece of the material that you would like the participant to read. Request that they review, or consider this material before attending the event. You might send a list of open-ended questions, getting them to recognize their challenges and or lack of knowledge. Another form of pre-work could be a book written by your guest speaker or on a topic applicable to your event.

Receiving a book makes the guest feel more of an obligation to fulfill his original commitment to you. A test or quiz can be helpful, considering they won't get the answers unless they attend the event. There are many different methods of pre-work, all of which enhance the commitment and sense of obligation to the participant.

> **All types of pre-work increase the participants' commitment and desire to attend your event.**

Let me give you a scenario. You are holding an estate-planning event. An available brochure lists the five most common mistakes that can affect family wealth. A week before the event, you call participants and let them know that to make the event more valuable you are sending a brochure. Request that they read the third paragraph on page three.

This does a number of things:

1. The participants realize you are serious about adding value.
2. It peaks their curiosity when you tell them to read just one paragraph, perhaps enough to read the whole brochure.
3. It makes the participant feel accountable.
4. It elevates their commitment to attending the event.

If you choose to send pre-work, it is absolutely critical that you address the pre-work at your event, in fact, at the beginning of the event. If you don't address it at the beginning, your guests will be constantly wondering when you are going to ask for their homework. I know it sounds a bit juvenile, but it's true. In addition, when you neglect to address the pre-work all together, many participants will leave angry or confused wondering why you asked them to do something in the first place.

> **The pre-work must be addressed and reviewed by the presenter at the beginning of the event.**

There are many ways to address the pre-work at the beginning of the event. In fact, by doing so you are better able to set a tone for interaction and communication. Think about your days in high school when the teacher asked who completed their work. Some raise their hand and some didn't. The people who raised their hand had an instant connection. So did the people who didn't. So, ask your guests the same question. You can then ask for feedback, "What did you learn from reading that article?" Now, tie the pre-work and discussion to the purpose of the event and guest speaker. This lends to a very smooth transition and sets up your presenter with guests anxious to hear what he or she has to say.

Whatever method you use, GET THE GUESTS INVOLVED. But remember, whatever you asked them to focus on should create a direct connection to the topic and event presentation.

> **Use the pre-work to engage the audience and create the importance of your guest speaker and their message.**

After creating the event, developing the invitations and receiving the RSVP's, so many advisors neglect the last and most important step: calling to confirm attendance the day before the event. This is so critical, yet most advisors fail to do it. Perhaps it's their fear of rejection getting in the way. They don't want to know if people aren't planning on coming. By being in denial you, one, lose the opportunity to engage in conversation with the prospect, and two, in many cases people just forget and need reminding. Just as we did when following up the invite, we want to make this a positive call. Sharing some piece of information that makes this event even more relevant to that client's particular circumstances can tip the scales on a guest that was straddling the fence.

> **Calling to confirm the day before the event can enhance your turnout and create another opportunity to profile your prospect.**

Remember, if you are excited about the event, your clients and prospects will be too. If you treat it like any other ho hum event, your clients and prospects will do the same. All of these steps not only enhance your participation level, but have a big impact on your ability to achieve your objectives. The more conversation you have with potential attendees, the more comfortable both of you will be when they arrive at your event. Everything we do is about developing and furthering relationships. Use your events to promote and encourage interaction.

**What you learned:**

- Both pre-work and confirmation calls increases your chances of achieving 100% attendance.
- All types of pre-work increase the participants' commitment and desire to attend.
- The pre-work must be completed and reviewed by the presenter at the beginning of the event.
- Use the pre-work to engage the audience and create the importance of your guest speaker and their message.
- Calling to confirm the day before the event can enhance your turnout and create another opportunity to profile your prospect.

# Chapter 9

## Step 8: Prepping the Presenter

**What you will learn:**

- **How to make your presentation support your objective**
- **How to be certain your presenter supports and encourages your objective**
- **How to coach your presenter**

The purpose of this chapter is to show you the importance of coaching your presenter to make certain that every part of the presentation leads to you achieving your primary objective.

Okay, you've selected a speaker with good presentation skills (you called a few references) who is also committed to supporting your event. The next step is to determine the message you want him or her to deliver. Remember, this is your event. Most guest speakers appreciate clear direction as to the message you want them to convey. It is your responsibility to provide the presenter with the guidance and information he or she needs to properly support your event.

An event should not be a series of isolated presentations, as if each person has his or her own agenda. There should be one main objective for the event supported by three master points. This way, every part of the presentation is connected and works together to achieve the predetermined goal. Many events have more than two speakers, making it even more critical to communicate your intentions to each presenter well in advance of the actual event. The best way to ensure that everyone involved with the program is clear on the focus and objective of the event is to provide a detailed agenda.

> **There should be one main objective for the event supported by three master points.**

In many cases, the three main points will come from the presenter. He or she is the expert in their field, which is why you have asked him or her to speak. Now you need to learn from them what could be your key points. By asking the presenter a series of questions, you can identify what would be most relevant to your tribal market and what topics would help you lead the participants to action. A few questions I might ask a presenter:

1. In the current environment, what would you consider the three biggest challenges for your clients?
2. What are the most common mistakes clients make in your field?
3. What is your best idea for your clients to take advantage of the current environment?

Notice, two of the questions focus on the current environment. This is important. Your presentation must be relevant to what your guests are experiencing today. By addressing current issues and challenges, you are better able to present a solution as well as the need to take action NOW. This process enhances your ability to move the participant to the next step, which may be to meet with you one on one.

From these questions, you should be able to develop the three master points, which will become the focus of your event. This focus will allow you to determine what exactly you want your guests to do next, what action you want them to take as a result of your presentation.

> **You want your three key points to be relevant to what your guests are experiencing today.**

As you can see from our sample agenda, the objective for the event is clearly spelled out and each participant understands what you are trying to achieve. The three key points highlight the message you intend the event to deliver to achieve the objective

## SAMPLE AGENDA

**Event:** The Power of Planning

**Objective:** To get the clients/prospects to sign up to have their legacy plans reviewed.

**Key Points:**

1. Legacy planning is a process that must continually evolve
2. Even the best of plans can have serious flaws
3. The power of a good legacy plan and the positive impact on the family

| 3:00 – 3:10 | Introduction and Welcome<br><br>1. Purpose of the presentation<br>2. What will be discussed<br>3. How it will impact you | Financial Advisor |
|---|---|---|
| 3:10 – 3:35 | The power of legacy planning<br><br>1. The pitfalls of most plans<br>2. The priorities of planning<br>3. The steps to success | Guest Speaker |
| 3:35 – 3:45 | Question & Answer Session | Guest Speaker<br>Financial Advisor |
| 3:45 – 3:55 | Conclusion<br><br>1. The impact of procrastination<br>2. The call to action<br>3. The motivation to change | Financial Advisor |
| 3:55 – 4:00 | Evaluations and Drawing | Financial Advisor<br>Assistant |

By focusing on the subject details, you will find that even the short presentations reflect three key points. I use the three key concepts not just in my events and presentations, but in my one-on-one presentations as well. You can provide the presenter with the key points, or discuss the objective for the event with him or her and ask them to provide their own key points that will tie into the presentation and help you achieve your goals. Either way, the guest speaker is now aware of your focus and desired outcome. This also shows the presenter that you are a professional and attentive to details.

There is nothing worse than a presenter who speaks way too long, throwing off the whole agenda and making the participants antsy. The sample agenda gives the presenter a better feel for the timing of the event and the role of each presenter. This implants the importance of timing in the mind of the presenter, and how he or she fits into the overall scheme of the event. This is valuable information, and gives him or her the ability to fine-tune the presentation to make it even more effective.

> **The sample agenda gives the presenter a better feel for the timing of the event and the role of each presenter.**

Here are examples that will give you some ideas for working with other presenters:

Mutual Fund/Professional Manager Wholesaler:

1. Overall sector performance
2. Their investment discipline and stock selection
3. Why this is a good investment today

Annuity/Insurance Rep:

1. The different types of products
2. Specific issues and benefits of this product today
3. For whom are these products most appropriate?

Professional Partners:

1. The typical challenges faced by clients in today's environment
2. The value they provide to their clients
3. Ways to prepare going forward

Exceptional Achievers:

1. What motivated you to take on this achievement?
2. What were the challenges you faced and how did you overcome?
3. What words of advice would you give for others?

Remember, the key points steer the participant to consider the topic at hand, how it applies to his or her life, and the importance of taking action.

**What you learned:**

- There should be one main objective for the event, supported by three master points.
- You want your three key points to be relevant to what your guests are experiencing today.
- The sample agenda gives the presenter a better feel for the timing of the event and the role of each presenter.
- The three key points drive the listener to action.

# Chapter 10
## Step 9: It's Show Time

**What you will learn:**
- How to lead the participants to action
- The three components to a great presentation
- How to create a receptive environment
- Ways to engage the audience
- How to add value while having fun
- The power of three
- How to elevate the audience to action
- How to capitalize on your evaluation

This is a big chapter, filled with a ton of valuable information. The purpose of this chapter is to help you understand how to make your event more effective. By utilizing these strategies, you will double and triple your results and increase the opportunity to achieve your event's objective and your long-term business goals.

At this point, you have created the foundation of your seminar strategy, based on the core needs and concerns of your tribal market. You have developed a defined process for attracting clients and prospects to your event. You have prepped your presenter and elevated the commitment of the participants. Our focus now shifts from filling the event to the event itself.

Now that you finally have them in the room, how do you move them to action? And, what action do you want them to take?

This is why having an objective is so important. To get participants to take action, you must create a sense of either fear or greed. Fear that if they don't take action they may suffer and greed that by taking action they have something to gain. This is an important factor when you are working with the presenter and focusing on your three key points. Not only is it important to identify the action you want them to take but during the presentation itself, it's important to create an atmosphere that encourages participation and comfort, and presents you as the provider of solutions.

There are two critical aspects to the presentation. When effectively combined they can be the catalyst to developing new business. First and foremost, create an environment that puts the participants at ease and has them interacting with others in the room. Let's call this seminar etiquette. Second is your presentation. There are three vital components to a great presentation:

1. Engage the audience
2. Educate the audience
3. Elevate the audience to action

In this chapter, you learn to create a warm, energized environment with your clients and prospects and to leverage that atmosphere by engaging the audience. You will also learn to educate the audience by providing just enough information to be of value, yet not overload them and dilute your message. Finally, you will learn to escalate the audience's commitment to taking action, specifically taking action with you. So, let's get started.

> **The three vital components to a great presentation:**
>
> 1. **Engage the audience**
> 2. **Educate the audience**
> 3. **Elevate the audience to action**

## It's Time to Party

Remember my guests who stayed at events long after the event and dessert ended? It wasn't really the dessert that made my events successful, it was the environment I created by engaging the audience before the event even started. The first step in creating a comfortable environment is to forget it's a seminar. Yes, you heard me; forget that this is a business affair.

> **Treat your event like you would a party.**

To effectively engage the audience in your event, you must treat it like you would a social affair or party – that's right, a party. Okay, we can forget the balloons and cake, but come with the same enthusiasm and energy.

Think about when you entertain in your home and invite guests. Usually, you invite guests with something in common – just like your event. What's the first thing you do when guests arrive? You greet them, take their coats, enjoy a few moments of light conversation, and then introduce them to the other guests in the room. A good host or hostess takes the opportunity to not just introduce their guests to each other by name, but will try and share something about them that would be of interest to others in the room. Just as we discussed in step five, this immediately creates an opportunity for the kind of conversation most people are looking for.

Think about your own experiences as an attendee at an event when you didn't know anyone sitting near you. You probably felt isolated and not terribly comfortable. Chances are, if the presenter did not engage the audience, you left the event feeling the same way. In reality, most people welcome the opportunity to become engaged in conversation. Sometimes they just need a little prompting or push.

Your seminar is no different. There is nothing worse than sitting at a table with other individuals you don't know, with nothing to do, not knowing what to say. Although many financial advisors recognize this discomfort, they remedy the problem by providing lots of brochures and reading material before the event. This is a mistake for two reasons. The individuals never really connect to your event because they pass their time focusing on the material. Second, many will go back to reading the material at some point during the presentation, which can be a huge distraction. Unless the material provides graphs, charts, or pictures intended to help the guests follow the presentation, leave the materials to the end of the event as the guests are walking out the door.

> **Leave most all of the marketing materials and brochures to be handed out at the end of the event.**

Now, I know I just told you not to hand anything out prior to the event not necessary for the presentation itself, but there is one exception. As your guests first sit down can be a perfect time to get undivided attention on your tri-fold brochure. I didn't say full presentation book or multi-page brochure; I said a small tri-fold brochure. Because this brochure is small and a quick read it, does not consume the participants' attention for long. This is possibly the one time people read your brochure.

Let's be honest, most of the time we hand or mail out our brochures, do you really think your recipients read it cover to cover? But at your event, your tri-fold brochure gives them just enough to read during those quiet moments. It gives them the opportunity to really take in what you have written, yet doesn't distract from your event or give them an out to forgo engaging in conversation. So, if you are planning to develop your own event program, this small brochure is a great piece that can actually help you promote your business.

> **Your tri-fold brochure can be a valuable marketing tool at your events.**

Now, let's go back to the topic at hand – making introductions. Make it easy for the guests to converse. Typically, people are more comfortable talking with one another when they have been introduced, so the introductions and information about the guests makes conversation more likely. Making strong introductions is critical to creating a warm and inviting atmosphere.

Consider the dinner party scenario. Once your guests arrive, you typically join the group, encourage conversation, and share interesting bits of information to keep the fires burning. If, at a dinner party, you are off preparing the meal, the energy of the group diminishes and conversation all but comes to a halt. So, the more time you spend engaging your guests, the better the momentum of the event. Otherwise, you become just an observer with little impact on the success of the evening.

> **Engaging your guests in conversation is critical to creating a warm receptive environment.**

## The Consummate Host/Hostess

Let's apply those concepts to your event. As your guests arrive, greet them with warmth and enthusiasm. Even if they are prospects, you can learn something about them with friendly conversation. Welcome your guests and lead them (not point them) to their table. Introduce them to everyone at the table, again dropping informational nuggets that intrigue everyone to engage in conversation.

Repeat this process until all of your guests have arrived and are seated at the table; then take a seat for yourself. Don't sit alone or stand in the back. Even if you plan to participate in the presentation itself, you want to sit with your guests.

We talked about this process in Chapter 6. I'm repeating the information now because I believe without this process of getting your guests to relax, you will lose a big percentage of the value of your events. If you realize this is something you are not comfortable with, just practice by applying the same skills to any social gathering you attend. Learn how to introduce your friends and associates in a way that makes them feel comfortable and engages them in conversation with each other.

> **Be sure to join your guests by sitting at the table with them.**

## Now Don't Be Shy

When all your guests have arrived and you have the opportunity to join them at the table, chances are most of the guests will be focusing on you. Take advantage of this opportunity to control the conversation. Regardless of how well you know all the individuals, treat them as if they are friends.

Now, for most of you, this may feel uncomfortable. Your preference will be to just put your toe in the water, perhaps by striking up conversation with just the person next to you. This is a time when you MUST go out of your comfort zone and cliff dive. Take the plunge. Trust me; the guests will welcome anything you have to say. If you know this will make you nervous, plan ahead. Come up with a topic that you believe to be important, something that was moving to you and share it. It's as simple as saying:

*"You know I just read an article in _____ that really made me think about..."*
Or
*"Last week I attended a presentation given by our chief economist and he shared some really interesting statistics, did you know that..."*

Be prepared to raise interesting topics of conversation pertaining to the seminar or some interesting fact or information regarding the markets or wealth management. Your guests will be looking to you to drive the conversation. Don't disappoint them. Not only will this approach create more comfort and conversation at your event, but it can be used in networking, cold calling, even in conversation with clients. Quite often, I have been at an event and during chitchat with a new guest, I would just dive in:

*"You know, I recently read an article that I can't seem to get out of my mind, did you realize…"*

This is a good opportunity to show your guests you are staying abreast of current events. It also opens the door to getting their thoughts. Once that happens, you are on your way. If you DON'T incorporate this strategy what will be different? Your guests remain uncomfortable; they converse only with those on either side of them. They continue to feel a bit isolated and maintain a protective or defensive mode; this does not bode well for your event.

> **Drive the conversation at your table by introducing an interesting story or article you recently read.**

The more comfortable they are, the more receptive they will be during the presentation. The more uncomfortable they are, the less receptive they will be, adding more tension to the air and stress to you. And, if you are trying to get them to take some kind of action, your chances of succeeding are much higher when they are relaxed and not threatened about sharing information.

Here are some examples:

*"Have any of you heard of ABC Management Company? I'm really excited about their presentation today because recently they've made some very interesting investments contrary to the markets. Does anyone here own a contrarian fund?"* (You can even go so far as to draw out a particular client who is usually more than happy to contribute.)

Another option:

*"You know, I heard the most fascinating report from our chief technology analyst this past week."* (Then begin sharing what you found so interesting about the future of technology. This will immediately entice others to comment as well.)

A third option:

*"How many of you currently own mutual funds? The manager we will be hearing from also manages a large portfolio of stocks..."*

When it is time to begin the event, be sure to excuse yourself so you can begin the proceedings. Leave a pen and paper at your place so when you return to your seat you can take note of interesting comments made by your guest speaker. These notes will be valuable to you after the presentation is completed.

## My Pet Peeve

I discussed this earlier in the book, but it is one of the most commonly overlooked aspects to events and it can single handedly derail your presentation. I know many of you do not like using a microphone. Often, the room seems small enough that you probably don't need one. Think again. You may think you are projecting, but when the room is filled, it can become difficult to hear above the luncheon noises. Furthermore, most voices fluctuate from low tones to higher pitches, especially when we are forced to project our voices. These fluctuations can make it difficult to hear.

We all have nuances to our presentation skills and frequently we have elderly people in the room who have begun to lose some of their hearing. Participants find it annoying when they have to struggle to hear a presentation. It makes it feel too much like work. It's better to be a bit too loud then to have your participants straining to hear you. Therefore, it is always better to use a microphone.

Many facilities now provide a lavaliere, or clip-on mike, that provides you with more freedom to move around as you speak. This flexible style can add to a more comfortable environment for your participants. And by all means, *don't* forget to test the equipment an hour before the event begins.

> **Unless you are sitting at a small table with less than ten people, plan on using a microphone.**

Okay, so now all your guests have arrived. You've taken some time to chat with all of them and engaged the whole table in some kind of discussion. It's now time to begin. The first and most important aspect to your presentation is getting the audience engaged from the beginning. There are many ways to do this that can be fun, easy to implement and highly effective.

## Step 1 – Engage the audience

Your first five minutes can be the catalyst to a successful event. They have a dramatic impact on the final results of the event. Getting the audience engaged in the topic helps them recognize why they want and need to be listening to the presentation. This same knowledge and experience can be tied into the end of the event, bringing your presentation full circle. There are many different ways to engage the audience:

- Demonstrations
- Games or quizzes
- True stories and testimonials

And, if properly managed, there is even a time and place for a little bribery. As with everything else we have discussed so far, the method you use to engage the audience has everything to do with the audience and the topic at hand.

> **Three ways to engage an audience:**
>
> - **Demonstrations**
> - **Games or quizzes**
> - **True stories and testimonials**

## Remember the Pre-Work?

If you gave the participants pre-work to increase their commitment to attending this event, then it is very important you follow thru and use the pre-work as a way to engage the audience. For instance, you could provide a simple quiz related to the pre-work for participants to complete before the event begins. As you review the quiz, ask those who answered 'yes' to a particular question to stand up and share their answer or experience. This instantly gets the audience engaged.

Recently, my clients, Tess and David Russell, from Merrill Lynch in Kentucky, held an event focusing on 401K fiduciary issues. All the participants were in charge of managing a company 401K plan. The purpose of the event was to help these individuals recognize the challenges that come from trying to keep up and comply with all the fiduciary rules and regulations.

To set the tone and to make the audience more receptive to the information, the Russells gave the participants a 5-question quiz. In each question, they were to rate their level of compliance on a scale of 1-5, five being extremely confident that they were in compliance on that particular issue. Then they totaled up the score they gave themselves for the five questions. David proceeded to ask who got a 25. Of course, no one stood up. He went down in numbers until there were participants that stood. At this point, he congratulated them.

This process helped the audience recognize that they were definitely NOT where they should be in terms of knowledge and compliance. David then shared with the audience that the purpose of the presentation was that they all leave with 25's, more knowledgeable and confident in their level of compliance. At the end of the presentation, David brought them full circle, referenced the quiz and applied this concept to the action they wanted the participants to take.

The way David and Tess started the event not only got the audience sharing and engaging in a discussion, but positioned them as experts who could provide the solution to the problems each of the participants were experiencing.

This quiz was a very effective process, but you must be careful how you draw people out and ask them to participate. No one likes to feel singled out for what they did wrong. You can single them out for what they did right.

When you have the advantage of identifying a participant who has accomplished what you are about to discuss, use this person as a testimonial or an expert during the presentation. This gives your presentation greater validity and usually people love to share what they know and have successfully accomplished.

> **Use your most knowledgeable and confident participant as a resource during your presentation.**

In addition to the pre-work, don't hesitate to bribe the participants. Begin early by rewarding those who participate. Consider using chocolate gold coins. They are easy to hold in your pocket and are very appropriate for a financial seminar. For great answers, hand out a mini 1000 Grand chocolate bar.

I've also seen presenters start their presentation with a sticky pad of one hundred $1.00 bills. As participants answered questions correctly, he tore off a $1.00 bill as a reward. This was a very fun and effective way to get the guests participating. It's amazing how much adults like to win prizes. Go to your local print shop with one hundred single dollar bills and ask them to create a pad of dollars. Odds are, you won't use up that many dollars and can use the same pad over and over again.

> **A little bribery goes a long way in encouraging participation.**

Another way to get the participants engaged is using play money. There are several ways you can do this. Distribute a fake bill to each participant, perhaps a 100 or 10,000 dollar bill. On the back of their bill, ask participants to write down their primary goal for investing. They can then leave the bill at their place, slip it in their pocket until you used to use it again in the program or they can put the bill into a bowl and you can randomly select bills and talk about how to achieve the goal. Odds are, the goals will amount to a few common items, growth, retirement, income, etc.

You can also have people select bills from a covered box, as they participate in the discussion. Each time they provide a comment, answer or raise a question, they get to pick a bill. By the end of the event, they can total up their money and the person with the most money wins a prize. This keeps the fun going throughout the event. As someone picks a bill there will be humorous comments when they draw a one, or they pick a $500 bill.

> **Use games familiar to your audience as a way to engage them.**

## Props and More Props

Another method of engaging the audience is using props. Props can be anything that creates a visual or ties your concept to something they can relate to in real life.

When I was working with women, although they felt challenged by the concepts of financial planning and asset allocation, I knew they had used those same concepts in managing their home, raising children, etc. They just needed to see and understand the correlation. One of the methods I enjoyed utilizing was, "The Game of Life," game board. Again, you must be very aware of your tribal market. Most of my clients were older women and were familiar with the Game of Life. Had I used a more recent game, it would have not had the same impact.

It's important that you ask the audience questions about the game, and by number of hands, identify who has played before. I would ask what is the objective of the Game of Life or, "how do you win?" The answer: by reaching the Millionaire Estates. I then asked, "How is that different from your objectives today?" I might ask, "What were some of the challenges you experienced along the path to the millionaire estates?" We talked about the game cards options, to buy insurance, get an education, deal with a catastrophe. My goal was to help them recognize that these are the same principles and concepts that we must apply to managing our own financial affairs.

To make this work, you MUST tie the game into the objective of the program. In fact, if you are using a game board as a prop, title the event in the same manner. An important factor to remember, if you start with The Game of Life, you must end with the Game of Life. Always come full circle.

Many other games can be used to emphasize a principle of investing; consider Battleship, Risk, Monopoly, Jeopardy, and so on. First, think about the principles you plan to address in your event. Determine which game best utilizes those same principles to win. Be creative. I think you will find that your events start to take on a more fun relaxed atmosphere, all because you used a little imagination and had some fun.

> **Always come full circle with your events tying the introduction to the closing presentation.**

Another method for engaging the audience is through demonstrations. Demonstrations are a great way to emphasize a concept. At one event I attended, the presenter used fake dollar bills all tied together in receding sizes. This demonstration started with a large bill and the impact of inflation on the size or value of that dollar.

You can also use props to emphasize a story, such as an old stock certificate. I've even used an outrigger paddle. Think out of the box and have fun.

## Make It Emotional

To set the tone, or to get your audience receptive to your presentation, use real-life testimonials. Real stories of actual events can be a powerful form of engaging the audience and getting buy-in. In fact, this is another method where the value goes beyond just seminars.

A real life testimonial can have a greater impact when prospecting or presenting to a potential client than any other sales tactic. As a financial advisor, you have stories you can tell of clients who experienced tremendous losses and crises as a result of not taking your advice. I often share the story of one of my first clients. Barbara was an artist. Through her divorce, she had a million dollars and no clue as to how to invest it. She was referred to me by another prospect. This was all the money she had to depend on for her retirement. Unless she hit it big with her art, she would not have much to support herself in her later years. Therefore, I invested her money with a conservative money manager. This, of course, was just before the tech bubble burst.

The manager produced stable returns averaging over 12% annually. But, when small cap managers were generating 100% returns, Barbara became disillusioned. Just six months before the markets crashed, she transferred her account to an independent advisor, specializing in over the counter and penny stocks. Before the transfer was complete, she asked me to do a few trades for her. I can tell you; these were far from blue chip stocks. Over the next twelve months, Barbara, who had nothing else for her retirement, lost 50% or more of her net worth, while her first money manager continued to generate positive returns.

This story has always elicited a sense of fear and concern. It also created greater buy-in with a potential prospect that might have been in a similar situation.

> **Sharing a real life story can stir the emotions and generate great buy-in.**

In addition to your own story, you can ask the audience if they know others with similar ones. A story coming from a participant increases the validity of your message. When sharing these stories, ask the audience, "What should this person have done differently? What was the mistake that was made?"

There are many different types of stories and testimonials you can choose:

- Historical stories of famous people. Estate planners often talk about Elvis Presley and Jackie Onassis, for example.

- Your own personal story; or something that occurred in your own family. This can be a particularly compelling method because it emphasizes that you are not in this business just to make money, but to save your clients from similar fates. For example, if your tribal market is business owners, because your parents were business owners, you might share how they invested every penny into their business and never for themselves. As a result, when they lost the business due to unforeseen factors, they had nothing left to fall back on. This really validates why you specialize in working with business owners and that you have an inside understanding of what a business owner experiences.

- A client testimonial (without disclosing who the client is). Sometimes these can be a conglomeration of a few scenarios pulled together. I know many FA's who share these stories and testimonials in emails and mailings as a way to illicit more interest in their business. Think about it. You get business letters all the time, but what if the letter started with, "Dear client/prospect: I wanted to share a real story with you that has compelled me to write this letter." The power of this mailer is in the story itself. Share why this story bothers you so much and that you are available to help others in the same situation.

- Another FA's client and experience (without disclosing who the client is). Perhaps you are new in the business and really don't have any great stories or experiences yet. Ask a fellow advisor. Just because it wasn't your client doesn't mean it didn't happen or that it isn't a real issue.

Here are a few sample testimonials provided by Robin Riendl a financial advisor in Anchorage Alaska:

## Divorcee

I recently received a referral of a woman who, at the age of 51, was facing an unexpected divorce. Although her attorney had already determined the division of assets, how she was going to manage those assets going forward caused her anxiety. Her only contact in the financial world was someone whom she considered "her husband's former advisor," who did not make her feel comfortable.

In meeting with her, my first objective was to uncover her level of knowledge and confidence in managing her financial affairs. To help her become comfortable with her own decision making process, we first discussed her philosophies, objectives, and future expectations. By consolidating all of her accounts, we were better able to develop and implement a simple wealth plan tailored to her investment strategy.

She now says she feels prepared and seems much more at ease about dealing with her financial situation. Although she has some decisions to make about her own personal direction, I continue to work with her to guide through ongoing financial decisions.

This is what I do. This is who I do it for.

## Sold Business

I recently met a 68-year old couple who had spent the bulk of their lives building a business that provided a quality life for them and their family. Although they were more than ready to start living their life, they were very nervous how to manage the sale of their business – their lifelong undertaking. For over 30 years, they invested most of their time, energy and money solely in their business, neglecting other aspects of their financial affairs. Now that they were going to depend on these assets for income, they realized their money had not been working as hard for them as they had worked to earn it. This caused them great concern.

After getting to know them and further discussing their plans for the future, we were able to develop a simple financial plan that alleviated their concerns and helped to provide them an understanding of how they could attain a comfortable lifestyle going forward. In our last meeting, they shared with me their photos of their recent trip with their grandchildren. Helping my clients reap the fruits of their labor and live the retirement they desire has been most rewarding.

This is what I do. This is who I do it for.

There are many ways to engage the audience. Your job is to pick a method that fits your tribal market, relates to your topic, and that you are comfortable presenting. Once you've engaged the audience and helped them recognize they may have a serious problem, we move to EDUCATE.

## Step 2 - Educate the Audience

One of the most common presentation mistakes, which can derail a whole event, is over-educating the audience. Too much information drowns the listener and eventually bores them to sleep, especially if you ramble.

> **Educating your audience becomes much easier if you have done a good job engaging the audience.**

Have you ever been to a seminar and later realized that it was difficult to articulate what you actually learned? Or, perhaps you left the event all fired up, with no idea what to do next. When was the last time you actually made a lasting change as a direct result of a seminar presentation? Here are two scenarios that can cause this failure of your event:

1. A presenter who is very motivational, but gives little to no applicable content. With this type of presentation, you leave the event feeling great, inspired to do better, but if asked what you actually learned or took away from the event, you struggle to find the words.

2. A presenter that is great at educating but as a result provide way too much information. This style dilutes

the message and prevents the participant from really recognizing the important points they were intended to walk away with.

The goal of a presenter is to provide both the motivation and inspiration to change or take action, with just enough education to validate the need to do business with you.

> **The goal of a presenter is to motivate AND educate.**

As presenters, we are compelled to share all we know, but the listener cannot absorb all we have to offer. Be selective and decide what you want the listener to walk away with. Narrow your directives to three key points. (There are those three key points again.) Three seems to be a magic number – four key points initiates diminishing returns; two key points isn't enough to make an impact or maintain the listener's attention. Focusing on three key points will keep the listeners focused and engaged.

> **Every presentation must be centered around 3 key points, not 2, not 4 but 3.**

## The Power of Three

In an earlier chapter, I gave examples of three key points based on products. Here are some additional examples based on process or topic-driven events:

Asset Allocation:

1. What is asset allocation?
2. The impact of poor asset allocation
3. How best to allocate your assets

Interest Rates:

1. The impact of rising interest rates
2. How to take advantage of rising interest rates
3. What you can do today

Women and Wealth

1. The statistics of women and wealth
2. The importance of becoming financially engaged
3. What you can do today

Family Wealth

1. The common pitfalls of family wealth management
2. The impact of proper planning
3. How to create a health family wealth plan

Since you have three key points to your event, your outside presenter will be responsible for delving into one of those points. For example, I may be holding a managed money presentation with a global money manager as the featured speaker. The following may be MY three key points:

1. The value of professional management
2. Why you should consider a global manager
3. Why this global manager

As you coach the presenter from the global management company, you can ask him to give you an additional three key points that address your second key point. If you put it all in outline form, it may look something like this:

1. The value of professional management (Your introduction)
2. Why you should consider a global manager (the managers presentation)
   a. Why international investing is important today
   b. How we select our portfolio of stocks
   c. How the performance has benefited the clients
3. Why this global manager (Your Conclusion and Wrap up)

## Step 3 - Elevating the Audience

It's now time to tie together information from the event and the educational parts of the presentation. Think of Step 3 as completing the circle; once you have closed the circle, you've captured the audience. In your conclusion, you want the flow to go something like this:

1. Emphasize the issue or areas of concern originally addressed in Step 1, or the engagement piece.
2. Summarize some of the key issues and points raised and addressed by the guest presenter in the educational piece.
3. Highlight what could happen if they don't take action toward global investing and the impact it could have on their financial future. By using testimonials of others who neglected this arena, you validate your message and make it real and tangible for the listener.
4. Accentuate the consequences of not addressing these areas of concern and create a sense of urgency that prompts the listener to action.

This is where your objective comes back into play. WHAT DO YOU WANT THE PARTICIPANT TO DO AS A RESULT OF THIS EVENT?

| By closing the circle, you capture the audience. |

Think about your event and your topic, and consider the action you want your participants to take. Typically, most financial advisors are looking for:

**Introduction Meeting:** This is an opportunity for prospects to come and visit with you in person. They're here to determine whether you can help them and if working with you is a good fit for the both of you. You are not pushing to get the account or making them feel pressured. You want to give the impression that not everyone is "qualified" to work with you. They must be "a good fit." This reduces the barriers that typically prevent the participant from committing to an appointment. It also creates a little motivation, as most people want to know they qualify. You could even change the title of this meeting to "30 minute coffee," or, "30 minute get to know you session." Make it sound less formal and more comfortable.

**Buy a product:** This action pertains to an event specifically associated with the value of one product. Creating some kind of time sensitivity or urgency dramatically enhances the client or prospect's desire to take action. Perhaps you can say that the presenter (professional manager) will only be in town for the next two days. "If you would like to schedule an appointment to learn whether this is an appropriate investment for you, sign up now." In most cases, they don't actually need to meet with the manager, you are really the deciding factor if it is a suitable investment for the client, but using the urgency of the manager leaving town adds to their motivation and need to take action.

**Refer a friend:** Perhaps your event is the last in a series of workshops. Your objective maybe two fold, to get the participants to schedule a meeting with you, AND to get more names into your database. In concluding this event, asking the participants to list three friends or colleagues that would like to receive invites to this same workshop can quickly multiply your lead/prospect list. Make it easy by handing out a form for them to fill in the names and contact information.

## It's Not a Sale

Don't think of your call to action as a sale; think of it as an opportunity to share your mission. Know exactly what you are trying to achieve for your clients and make them recognize that most investors have not done all they should to grow, preserve, and transfer their wealth. Additionally, make them conclude that by not working with you they may be at risk.

Believe it, present it, and they will come.

## A Missed Opportunity

Most financial advisors assume that once you have concluded your event, your guests will naturally get up and leave. That seems especially true when you are the presenter in front of the room concluding the event.

In fact, it does not have to be this way. By understanding the nuances of working your table, you will find your guests and yourself enjoying another cup of coffee, while your table discussion continues long after everyone else has gone home. In order to capitalize on this opportunity, there are three very important factors that you must adhere to:

1. **You must be willing to turn people away.** It's important that you sit at the table with your guests. Having an overflow of guests is a good thing, but when it means you have to host two tables, you lose the connection with your guests that is so important.
2. **Take notes on the presentation.** By taking notes on the presentation, you now have specific topics of conversation to engage your table in conversation.
3. **Serve coffee with great desserts.** Be sure the desserts are served as the event is concluding. This encourages your guests to linger a bit, giving you time to get the conversation started.

At the beginning of this book, I shared my preference for smaller events. Let me clarify what I mean by that and why. A smaller event, if used effectively, creates more intimacy. By engaging a smaller group of people, you are better able to gather more pertinent and personal information about each prospective client. Your level of intimacy accelerates your ability to open accounts.

In order to capitalize on this concept, I found it was important to sit at the table with my guests. By sitting with them, I become one of them. If my event was too large, I would only be able to sit with a handful of my guests, making it appear as if I was ignoring the others. As a result, when the event was over I would have to stand up to thank the other guests for coming. Once I stood, it's as if I just gave the guests at my table permission to leave. Therefore, I learned early on that it was better for me to turn away guests who called to RSVP, if I would end up with more (including myself) than could sit at one table.

There turned out to be another advantage of limiting the number of guests. When people called to RSVP, I did not hesitate to tell them my event was full if I knew it meant overflowing into a second table. I would capture their information and have an opportunity to engage them in further conversation. More importantly, by turning them away, my events appear to be in great demand, which was great image to project.

Another factor that added to my clients staying and re-engaging in conversation was taking notes. Whenever I had a guest presenter, I would take notes while sitting at the table with my guests. At the end of the presentation, I now had specific topics of conversation to discuss with my guests, re-engaging them.

## Gaining Their Commitment

So, we've talked about the action we want our participants to take, but how do we actually get them to do what we want? There are many different methods in getting guests to commit to an action, such as passing around a sign-up sheet or having an assistant at the door handing out your calendar.

However, I've found most of these methods generate lackluster results. I prefer to ask the client for some type of commitment and combine this commitment with the evaluation form for the event. This leads me to…

## The Dreaded Evaluation

Have you ever looked forward to filling out an evaluation form? The only time I ever want to fill one out is when the experience was miserable. Then I readily shared my thoughts. After sitting through a long event with a boring presenter, I look forward to giving my opinion. Usually, when someone hands me a full-page evaluation form, I hear myself saying "Ugghhhh! What is motivating me to take the time and energy to complete this form?"

That is not the way I want to end my events. Still, it is important to know how the event went. What is it we really want to know?

The kind of information we want to draw from the participants should be about the value the participant gained from attending the event. These types of questions add value to the participants, while also giving you the feedback you want on the impact of the event.

However, the process I'm about to share with you will do even more than that. You will capture the contact information of each participant, at the same time providing yourself with tremendous material to work with when following up with the participant after the event.

## Packing a Punch

I created an evaluation form that is simple, yet packs a powerful punch. The form is less than half an 8½ x 11 sheet. Rather than listing multiple-choice questions or a numbered ranking system, I list three open-ended questions that when completed, give me more information than I would have gathered from any technical evaluation.

One questions should always be, "What do you intend to do as a result of this event?" Regardless if the answer is to meet with you or just to gather their documents together, you should feel good that the event motivated these individuals to take another step towards properly managing their financial lives. The reality is, if they actually do complete their action step, they will consider you as a positive catalyst. So, for now let's change the title from, "Evaluation Form," to, "Action Form."

How you present the action form can also impact the results. There are a number of ways to incorporate your action form during your event. For starters, you can place one at each person's place before the guests arrive. If you do this, it is important that you address the form during your introductory comments. Be sure to explain the purpose of the form and, as always, "WIFM" (What is in it for me?).

1. First, explain why you are hosting this event.
2. Share how important it is to you that they walk away from this event with an actionable idea. Stress that although this event may be fun, it is important to you that the participants leave with the value you intend.
3. Ask them to look at the action form. "This form will help you solidify what you learned here today and what you intend to do as a result (The WIFM).
4. Tell them your strong desire to see them move forward as a result of this event. You will follow up with them and hold them accountable to their action.
5. Let them know you're giving this to them at the beginning of the event so that as they learn something particularly useful, they can jot it down immediately instead of waiting until the end of the presentation.

6. Finally, at the end of the presentation, once they have completed this action form, ask them to fold it up and you will collect them as a drawing for... (gift basket, book, etc.)

You can adapt this script to be used at the end of the presentation, if you like. Either of these approaches can be effective. What is important is how you tie it into your presentation. Emphasize your commitment to making sure they walk away with something valuable.

Recently, my clients in Kentucky, Tess and David Russell, gave a retirement presentation to HR and CPA's. Their intent was to generate more referrals, but also to impress the participants with the added value they would provide if their company or client were to become their client as well. Here are the three questions they asked of their participants:

1. What was the most compelling piece of information delivered to you today?
2. What is your biggest concern regarding your retirement plan?
3. What will you do different with your plan as a result of attending this summit?

Here is another example and how the form can be positioned. Notice the simplicity.

## SAMPLE EVALUATION FORM

Name: _____

Phone: _____

Email: _____

1.  What was the most valuable idea you gained from today's presentation?

2.  What change or action do you plan to take as a result of this event?

3.  What are your most pressing financial concerns at this time?

When participants see this simple form, they are much more receptive to filling it out, especially since you have validated the importance to them.

> **Keep your evaluation form simple.**

If an evaluation of the technical aspects of the presentation is what you are after, ask one or two people – guests, colleagues or friends – to attend your event solely for the purpose of evaluating the technicalities of the event.

## Follow up

One of the most neglected aspects of an event program is participant follow-up. It is critical that the very next day after the event, you reconnect with the participants. This small evaluation form will provide you with information allowing you to immediately initiate meaningful conversation. Don't underestimate the impact this evaluation can have on the results of the event and future of your business.

**What you learned:**

- The three vital components to a great presentation:
    - Engage the audience
    - Educate the audience
    - Elevate the audience to action
- Treat your event like you would a party
- Leave most of the marketing materials and brochures to be handed out at the end of the event.
- Your tri-fold brochure can be a valuable marketing tool at your events.
- Engaging your guests in conversation is critical to creating a warm receptive environment.
- Be sure to join your guests by sitting at the table with them.
- Drive the conversation at your table by introducing an interesting story or article you recently read.
- Unless you are sitting at a small table with less than ten people, plan on using a microphone.

- Three ways to engage an audience:
  - Demonstrations
  - Games or quizzes
  - True stories and testimonials
- Use your most knowledgeable and confident participant as a resource during your presentation.
- Be sure the exercise you use to open the presentation and engage the audience ties into one of your key points.
- A little bribery goes a long way in encouraging participation.
- Use games familiar to your audience as a way to engage them.
- Always come full circle with your events, tying the introduction to the closing presentation.
- Sharing a real life story can stir the emotions and generate great buy-in.
- Educating your audience becomes much easier if you have done a good job engaging the audience.
- The goal of a presenter is to motivate AND educate.
- Every presentation must be centered around 3 master points, not 2, not 4 but 3.
- By closing the circle, you capture the audience.
- Imply that prospects must qualify to become your client.
- Present a reason that will encourage the guest to buy a product now.
- Ask the participants to list three friends/colleagues that would like to receive invitations to future events.
- Ways to make sure your guests linger after the event:
  - Be willing to turn people away
  - Share your notes from the presentation
  - Provide a decadent dessert
- Be sure to sit at the same table as your guests.
- Your evaluation should provide you with valuable information that clarifies the impact your event had on the participant.
- Your evaluation form should contain just three open-ended questions.
- Keep your evaluation form simple.

# Chapter 11

## Step 10: Going for the Goal

**What you will learn:**

- The importance of follow-up
- How to turn your follow-up in to a profiling opportunity
- How to track your progress
- How to know when they are milking you
- How to benefit from accurate statistics

The purpose of this chapter is to demonstrate the importance of the follow-up process and show you how to track your events to increase your overall results.

You've spent weeks, maybe even months, planning and preparing for your event. You had good attendance and completed the presentation well. Now comes the defining moment – closing for business. The post-event activity, also known as the follow-up process, is the single most critical component to achieving your objectives and closing the business. As critical as this step is to getting results, most advisors neglect to do it.

> **Not following up on your event is like dropping the ball on the 10-yard line.**

## Don't drop the ball

You worked so hard to get to this point. You have high expectations that the event will grow your business. With so much riding on the success of the event, why do we consistently fumble on the 10-yard line? Is it fear of success? Fear of rejection? Is it just downright laziness? Or, is it that we just don't really have an effective follow-up process?

By incorporating the simple action form into your event, you have already developed an effective means of following up. The act of following up is not just important, it is essential to getting the business.

The first step is making the call immediately after the event, but before you pick up the phone, you must plan how to approach the participant and drive them to do business with you.

Here is an example of a typical follow-up process: You call the guest, thank him or her for attending your event, and then ask if you can help with their investments. Okay, maybe your follow-up isn't exactly like that, but I bet it's pretty close. Here's the problem – **why the heck are you thanking *them* for coming?** If you followed my event process from start to finish, *they* should be thanking *you*.

Think about the last time you attended a seminar by choice. Let's assume you attended a Tony Robbins event. Is Tony going to call to thank you for attending? No. Chances are, you'll want to thank him for providing you with valuable information that will change your life. The same should go for your events. If you follow this process, you will be adding tremendous value and your clients will thank YOU.

> **Your guests should be thanking you for the value you have added to their financial future.**

Let's take this a step further. If Tony Robbins did call you after attending one of his events, how do you think that call would go? Tony's objective is to change lives; therefore, his goal would be to learn how his event impacted your life and what you are going to do about it. He might even recommend that you attend an additional workshop in order to get the most from the first event, and increase your ability to achieve your goals. This whole conversation would be swept up in Tony's unbridled passion for what he does, how he can help you and what you need to do next.

Apply that same concept to your own events. You provided your attendees with valuable information that could have a tremendous impact on their lives and their financial future. You are excited they came and are looking to improve their lives. Your objective is to inspire and motivate them to take the next step. Your action form gives you the information and the tools to engage in a compelling conversation that reinforces your value and the benefits to the client.

When making your follow up call, use the following process:

1. **Share your excitement** that they were able to attend the event. Comment on any questions they may have asked or their participation during the presentation.
2. **Describe what you found** to be the most valuable part of the event. Don't be afraid to share what YOU learned. No one expects you to know everything and this humble approach resonates with prospective clients.
3. **Treat the prospect as if they were your client.** Ask questions about their portfolio and how these "lessons" apply to them and their current investment plan.

4. **Share what you believe** are the risks of not taking action.

5. **Ask them how they intend to avoid the risks**, or how they plan to take advantage of the opportunity.

Your script may go something like this:

*"Mr. Prospect, I'm so glad you were able to make this event. I was very impressed with the presenter and found his comments on the Japanese markets quite interesting. Your question about _____ seemed to be right on the money." (This should instigate conversation.) "In your evaluation, you mentioned you found the statistics on Japanese companies exceeding expectations very interesting. Why does that interest you? How are you currently invested in the Japanese markets? What other international markets are you optimistic about? On your action form, you talked about exploring other types of international managers. Tell me, what's your current allocation?"*

There will be times that you don't have the benefit of the action form. In that case, consider the following script:

*"Mr. Prospect, I'm so glad you were able to make this event. I was very impressed with the presenter and found his comments on the Japanese markets quite interesting." (This should instigate conversation.) "Mr. Prospect, what was the most valuable piece of information you took away from this event? How does that apply to your situation? Wouldn't it make sense for us to sit down and review your portfolio to be certain?"*

## Are You Running a Non-Profit?

By referring to the action form, you have an immediate advantage because you already know the prospect's areas of interest. Remember to keep your objective in mind. If you are looking for referrals, ask for referrals. If you want an appointment, ask for an appointment. Or, if you are looking to close a sale, ask for the order. Remember, you just provided your client or prospect with an opportunity to learn valuable information while enjoying a nice lunch. You are not running a non-profit and they know it.

> **Your Action Form provides you with a tremendous advantage when following up with your guests.**

## Tracking Your Progress

Six months has past and you have held at least one seminar a month. It's time to look back and evaluate your progress. How many new accounts have you opened? How many referrals have you generated because of your events? How many new assets have you uncovered and how much commission have you generated due to your events and topics?

Do you know?

Most financial advisors do a very poor job of keeping track of the impact their events have on their business. Most of the time, the benefits are not immediately noticeable. Some of the value of holding events is in generating referrals or introductions to more potential clients. If you don't keep track of this information, you may never appreciate the true value these events are having on your practice.

An effective tracking system is the only way to honestly measure how well your events are impacting your business. It doesn't have to be overly complicated or challenging. The key is finding a system that works for you and covers the areas that are important to you.

> **By tracking your events, you are better able to recognize how they are helping to grow your business.**

When I was hosting my events, I had a binder with monthly tabs. Each of my events had its own page (this was before we were proficient with computers). As investors called to RSVP, I added their name to that particular event page.

It was a simple method and my sales assistant knew where the binder was and could enter names when I wasn't available. This was also the list I used to call and confirm attendance.

Over time, I went back through the binder, event by event, to highlight those guests that eventually opened accounts with me. What I didn't do, and would do today, is record those that also brought guests. This is a very important factor. Those clients that continually bring friends and are constantly introducing me to new investors, I want to recognize and show my appreciation. Clients and prospects that help you continue to fill your pipeline are just as valuable as a participant that opens an account.

I also learned from this process that, typically, a prospect would attend three of my events before they would open an account. Three again seemed to be the magic number. This helped me to better manage my own expectations as to opening accounts. It also gave me a way to regulate when it was time to close business.

> **By tracking your events, you are better able to manage your own expectations.**

I began using the third event as my regulator. If a prospect had attended three events and had not yet committed to doing business with me, then this was my opportunity to draw a line in the sand and get a commitment or cut bait.

Not tracking your event progress is like trying to become a great athlete and never reviewing your game stats. It's easy for us to see what we want to see. For those whose glass is typically half-empty, recognizing all the positive aspects that come from your events will keep you moving forward and motivated. For those with the glass half full, tracking your progress will force you to identify when something is not working and you are not making progress. Either way, tracking your record is essential if you want your events to grow your business.

> **Tracking your progress is essential to a successful event program.**

In today's world, technology makes the tracking process easy. You can keep it simple, tracking business generated and referrals or introductions received, or you can make it more technical, focusing on each event, the title, the number or participants even the client/prospect ratio etc. The key is how detailed you want and need it to be. In my case, if the process is too detailed, I have a tendency to avoid it and let it slip through the cracks. Yet I have many clients (financial advisors) who thrive on the details and statistics. The important thing is find a tracking system that works for you.

## Are They Milking You?

Another benefit of tracking your events is recognizing when someone is taking advantage of you. Odds are, because your events are small, participants can't as easily get lost in the shuffle. In addition, when you host events at a high-end location, you tend to attract people that are more seriously interested. When participants recognize the high cost of an event, they are less apt to take advantage. Even considering those factors, you still find some people who will justify using your events for their own benefit.

To prevent this, try these steps:

First, by phoning each participant, you have the ability to qualify him or her over the phone. If your event is at an upscale venue where you are providing lunch, you have every right to qualify those who have committed to attend. If a guest hesitates to provide you with information, or becomes offended by your questions, odds are you just saved yourself paying for their lunch. Again, to qualify you don't have to go into detail. Simply clarify to whom this event is most suited. Asking if they fit those criteria is all you may have to do.

> **Know when to draw a line in the sand.**

Second, if you are tracking your events, you will know when someone has come more than once. If after the second event, you are still unable to engage the guest in a meaningful conversation, consider deleting them from your invite list.

So, what if they've attended three events and have not opened an account with you? Perhaps they haven't opened an account but have introduced you to three new prospects that came as guests? Should you allow this person to continue coming? By maintaining accurate information, you are better able to make these decisions, to know that you are progressing toward your goal and that you are not being taken advantage of by any of the participants.

During my event program, there was a woman who attended a number of my events yet had not opened an account. At first, I didn't mind her coming because she raved about me to the other participants and created a very positive environment. Eventually, I realized I had to draw a line in the sand. This was my first real experience with someone who might be taking advantage of my event program.

So, I bit the bullet and confronted her. I told her that I loved her coming to my events, she was a positive influence, but the fact was these events were primarily for my existing clients and those that intend to open accounts with me. She then offered to send me some money so that she could open an account. Of course, she only offered to send me $1,000. Yes that's right, one thousand dollars, with the expectation that when her property sells (and the check is in the mail) she will transfer in more.

At this point, I realized what was going on and told her that I really couldn't help her with just one thousand dollars and thanked her for the offer. She never came to another event and I guess she never sold her property because I never heard from her again. An inexpensive lesson learned. This incident really started me tracking how many times individuals attended my events.

On the next page is a tracking template I created. This template allows you to track how many events each individual attends and what you generated because of their participation in referrals, assets, and gross revenues.

In addition, this template helps you track the events that generated the most interest and the events that generated the greatest amount of business. This may seem somewhat cumbersome, but keeping accurate statistics on the results of your events not only provides you with valuable information to reinforce what's working, but can be a tremendous marketing tool when looking for sponsors and partners with a budget.

# TRACKING REPORT

| Client | Account opened | Appts | Referrals | Assets Uncovered | Gross | Sept. 15, 05 | | 10-Oct-05 | | 12-Nov-05 | |
|---|---|---|---|---|---|---|---|---|---|---|---|
| | | | | | | RSVP'd | Attended | RSVP'd | Attended | RSVP'd | Attended |
| Mary Smith | | 1 | | $240,000 | | X | X | X | X | X | X |
| John Brown | | | | $40,000 | | X | | X | | X | X |
| Suzie Q | | | | | | | | | | | |
| | | | | | | | | | | | |
| | | | | | | | | | | | |
| | | | | | | | | | | | |
| | | | | | | | | | | | |
| | | | | | | | | | | | |
| | | | | | | | | | | | |
| | | | | | | | | | | | |
| | | | | | | | | | | | |
| | | | | | | | | | | | |
| | | Total Appts | | | | Total RSVP'd | Total Attended | Total RSVP'd | Total Attended | Total RSVP'd | Total Attended |
| | | 1 | | | | 2 | 1 | 2 | 1 | 2 | 2 |

**What you learned:**

- Not following up on your event is like dropping the ball on the 10-yard line.
- Your guests should be thanking you for the value you have added to their financial future.
- Be excited and enthusiastic when making your follow up calls.
- Your action form provides you with a tremendous advantage when following up with your guests.
- By tracking your events, you are better able to recognize how they are helping to grow your business.
- By tracking your events, you are better able to manage your own expectations.
- Tracking your progress is essential to a successful event program.
- Know when to draw a line in the sand.

# Chapter 12

## Dress Rehearsal

**What you will learn:**

- **Why your appearance is so important**
- **The impact of inappropriate attire**
- **How to get help**

In this chapter, you will learn the importance of your appearance so that you can ensure you look great and attract success.

Everything we do leading up to this event helps you achieve your goals and reach your objective. The topic, guest speaker, invitations and venue all play a role. The presentation, the evaluation forms and the follow-up are all geared toward enhancing your ability to achieve your goals and objectives. The last thing we want is something to create a distraction and negate all the effort we have worked so hard to put into place. Your appearance at the event is no different. What you wear can either make or break your event.

When considering what to wear, think carefully. The most important thing is not to create any distractions to your message. You want to be sure you blend in with your tribal market yet still maintain a sense of your own personality. It's a bit easier for men when it comes to what to wear; a traditional suit with a somewhat conservative tie will do nicely. You don't have to hide your personality, but you don't want to force it on the participants. Leave the cartoon ties at home.

> **What you wear can either make or break your event.**

For women, there is less of a standard for professional attire, which leaves a lot more room for error. Have you ever been to an event where the presenter is constantly messing with her hair? Perhaps she has one of those hairstyles that covers half her face. What about when the presenter wears some dangling earrings that continue to bob back and forth while she speaks? And of course, there is nothing worse than a top that reveals too much or a skirt that is too short. All of these create a tremendous distraction to your audience and minimize the importance of your message.

When choosing what to wear, you must consider a number of factors. One, you want to be comfortable. (A pair of baggy sweats or jeans is too comfortable.) Two, you want to feel powerful and confident. When you look sophisticated you act sophisticated. When you are confident in how you look, you will appear confident to the audience.

Be stylish but not trendy. Remember we are in the financial services business. You are trying to impress your audience and build their confidence in your ability to manage their life savings. Think about it. What would you want a person to look like if you were going to hand them millions of dollars to manage for your family wealth?

> **Your appearance should increase the participants' confidence in your ability to manage millions of dollars.**

Avoid these common presenter faux pas. When you do, you enhance the impression you are trying to make on the participants and reduce the risk of distraction. Remember, you want them to talk more about what you said then what you wore.

- **Wear a suit:** Always wear a suit unless you are at a golf course or extremely casual location, where a suit may be out of place. A suit is not a pair of slacks with a similar jacket. A suit is two pieces, purchased together, typically made of the same material. Colorful separates, if properly coordinated, can be appropriate but a suit has more polish.
- **Make it appropriate:** Keep hemlines down and necklines up. You certainly don't have to look frumpy, but a few inches above the knee is high enough for your skirt. As for your top, if you're concerned about what someone would see if you leaned forward, then think again. I'm not talking turtlenecks, but an appropriate top or blouse that covers all the essentials. You don't want to upstage the women in the audience and you want the men thinking of you managing millions of dollars, not acting as hostess at a party.
- **Style your hair professionally:** There is nothing more annoying than watching a woman continuously tucking her hair behind her ear, or seeing only half her face because her hair keeps hanging down. Don't wear excessive bows or clips in your hair; you don't want to distract the audience. If you color your hair, be sure it looks fresh and up-to-date. Your hair can be both stylish and neat, requiring little or no fiddling.

- **Look put together:** Make sure that your accessories all match or compliment your outfit. Jewelry can enhance an outfit and give a more worldly sophisticated impression. The wrong jewelry however, can overwhelm an outfit and draw all the focus away from your message. Scarves are a great addition if worn properly and match with your suit. Coordinated (but comfortable) shoes are important for both appearance and performance. Make sure they look new and are not worn and scuffed. And please, don't wear colored hose, keep it neutral.

> **To play the part, you must act the part – Look like you can manage millions of dollars.**

If you do not feel confident in the area of fashion, try these techniques:

1. Watch the female newscasters on TV. Notice what you like and what you don't. Do you find yourself focusing on what they are wearing or listening to what they have to say? Observe their makeup and any accessories. They definitely want you paying attention to what they have to say without distracting you with their attire.

2. Talk to a fashion coordinator at your local upscale department store. They can help you begin building a base of outfits. Overtime and with more experience, you can interchange outfits so you are always looking sharp and sophisticated. I especially enjoy working with the staff at Nordstrom's.

Remember, in the financial services industry, it's always better to err on the conservative side.

**What you learned:**

- **What you wear can make or break your event.**
- **Your appearance should increase the participants' confidence in your ability to manage millions of dollars.**
- **To play the part, you must act the part – Look like you can manage millions of dollars.**

# Chapter 13
## Love What You Do

The reality is, seminars are not for every financial advisor. If you don't enjoy it, odds are it won't work for you and your business. This has nothing to do with your ability as a financial advisor; it just isn't a prospecting method that fits your style and personality. Knowing it's not a good method for you is just as valuable as knowing that it is.

> **If you don't enjoy it, then don't do it.**

A good seminar program can help to sustain the growth of your business forever. As long as you continue to track your results, evaluate your progress and adapt to the times and economic climate, your seminar program will become a referral machine creating a steady stream of new business far surpassing your original goals.

A consistent seminar program keeps you continually connected with your clients, discussing topics relevant to the times. More important, your clients feel as if they are members of a club. By getting to know you better and becoming more comfortable interacting with your other clients, you give your clients an exclusive environment with you as the hub of the wheel.

> **A seminar program can feed the growth of your business for life.**

However, if you find this process of creating seminars to be drudgery and a tremendous amount of work, perhaps this is not what you were meant to do.

The only thing that can prevent this seminar program from succeeding is you – that's right -- YOU. It won't be the venue, the invite, or the presentation that lacks effectiveness. If you don't enjoy the seminar process, you will struggle to get good results regardless of whether you follow every step in this book, complete all the assignments, and execute all the directives. This does not mean you are a failure, it just means seminars are not one of your strengths.

People are successful with seminars not just because they developed a thoughtful program, but because they LOVE IT. They love the challenge of thinking up new events. They love the creativity that comes with the marketing, and they love every opportunity to engage with their clients/ prospects. They enjoy improving their presentation skills, and they love the sense of accountability that an event program creates. Knowing they have a commitment to a deadline increases their desire to progress with their practice.

When you enjoy the process, your guests hear and feel your energy, your enthusiasm, and your commitment to their welfare. Your passion brings you success.

When you love what you do, it becomes effortless. You feel more energized, you ooze passion, and your confidence builds on itself until you become a magnet for success. The same holds true with your seminar program. As your event program develops, you will find it easier to identify good speakers. You will quickly recognize a good location for an event. As the environment changes, so too will the issues. Having a well developed event program allows you to continually address the changes in the business and financial arena.

> **A well-developed seminar program allows you to continually evolve with the financial landscape.**

Let go of all those preconceived ideas about how to build a business. Everything has changed in our business. Though there are valuable lessons to learn from past successes and mistakes, it's important to take a fresh look at your world today. Building trusting relationships is a critical component to future business. Creating attractive opportunities for prospective clients to see you and experience what you have to offer accelerates the relationship process.

Seminars are not just a great way to get in front of new prospective clients, but also to provide valuable education and information to your clients, who in-turn will market you and your events. Consider re-thinking your role as a financial advisor, and the power and influence you have over the future wellbeing of your clients. Recognize the impact your seminar program can have on your business.

Remember to have fun, be creative, stick with the program, and watch your business grow. Don't fight your compliance issues, work with and around them. A few changes to your seminar title will not deter someone from coming. What is more important than the language of your invites is the continuity and repetition of your events.

> **Make it fun but stick to the game plan.**

In the remainder of this book you will find worksheets from previous chapters and assignments, as well as sample invitations, scripts, letters and emails. I've even included a post event evaluation sheet that can add tremendous value as you continue to improve your events.

The sample materials that follow have been provided by advisors, just like you, who have developed event programs of their own. They were willing to share some of the materials that worked for them. Again, these are samples or examples of what you can do. It's important that you take these pieces and make them your own. Give each piece your own personal touch and style so that it works for and reflects YOU and focuses on your tribal market.

> **Follow the model but make it your own based on you and your tribal market.**

In closing, I hope you enjoy hosting events as much I did. I loved the opportunity of creating new ideas and topics. I relished the opportunity to meet new people, to engage them in conversation and to encourage them to better their lives by attending my event. I loved the value my event program had in building my business. It was a natural fit for me and my level of energy but most importantly, it created a way for me to meet and speak to five new prospects each week without spending interminable hours on the phone (hours I didn't have) cold calling perfect strangers.

To your seminar success,
Adri Miller-Heckman

# Sample Invitations

# Save the Date!

# *A Women's Perspective to Family Wealth and Values*

At Smith Barney we understand the financial challenges you face as a woman, wife and mother. With that in mind I have developed a women-only series of events designed to address the many financial complexities families face from the women's perspective.

## September 28th
### *The Financial Facts of a Women's Life; What every Women Should Know*

## October 26th
### *The Art of Surviving Wealth*

## November 16th
### *A Family Plan: Putting you and your team Together*

Hosted by:

**Linda E. Hoffman**
**Cordially invites you to attend**

## *"Women Breaking the Mold"*

Featuring

**Madeline Slavin**
**Mountaineer**
Her Adventures as a Woman Climbing Mt. McKinley.

and

**Linda E. Hoffman**
**Second Vice President – Financial Consultant**
Success Comes From a Plan and a Process

Friday, September 16, 2005
11:30 - 1:30 pm
370 17th Street, Ste. 2800  Denver, CO
Republic Plaza Building (on Tremont, between 16th & 17th)

*Lunch will be $11.00 per person*

## Guests are Welcome

RSVP to:

**Glenn Louie,**
**Financial Consultant**
**Smith Barney**

**Cordially invites you and a guest to attend a special**
**dinner discussion**

**Exclusively for clients:**

# *"Bridging the Longevity Gap"*

*STRATEGIES AND VEHICLES TO HELP MAINTAIN YOUR*
*INCOME LEVEL THROUGHOUT YOUR RETIREMENT*

**Wednesday, October 19, 2005**
**6:00 p.m.**

**The 555 American Steakhouse**
**Grand Prix Room**
**555 East Ocean Boulevard**
**Long Beach, California**

Seating is very limited for this discussion.
Please RSVP to Marla Meckes at

# SMITH BARNEY
## citigroup

INVITES YOU TO A SPECIAL DISCUSSION ON

# THE CHANGING DYNAMICS OF GLOBAL AND REGIONAL OIL AND GAS MARKETS

WITH

# Dr. Dennis O'Brien

**Dennis O'Brien is a widely recognized leader in the international energy industry. He provides weekly commentary on fuels prices and energy markets to several media outlets and is frequently quoted by the local, national, and international press.**

Hosted by:

## Doug Bruton
### Financial Advisor
### Smith Barney, Citigroup

**(Contact info here)**

# Wise Women and Wealth

## Save the Date
Friday, October 28
11:30am to 1:30pm

# Identity Theft; Are you at Risk?

Do you carry a purse?  Is your Social Security number in your wallet?  Do you receive numerous credit card solicitations in the mail?  Do you use a strip shredder?

This workshop teaches you how certain habits can increase your risk for identity theft.  You'll learn what you can do to reduce your risk, as well as what steps to take if your identity is stolen.

## (ADVISOR)

2ND VICE PRESIDENT – INVESTMENTS
FINANCIAL CONSULTANT
PHONE:

Whether you are an experienced wine connoisseur or a novice,

## The Lake Avenue Group at Smith Barney

Invites You to join us at

### The Nose

For a celebration of wine!

Monday, March 13th, 2006

6:00 - 8:00PM

Light Hors d'oeuvres will be served

Please feel free to bring friends!

**The Nose Wine Cellar**

696 E. Colorado Blvd.  Shop 6

Pasadena, CA  91101

# *Wise Women and Wealth*

### "Protecting your Pocket Book"

Featuring

## Linda E. Hoffman

2nd Vice President – Financial Consultant

### *"Long Term Care Insurance; is it appropriate for you?"*

And

## Lisa Curtis

Director, Consumer Services
Office of the District Attorney

### *"Common habits that are increasing your risk for identity theft."*

Friday November 4, 2005
11:30am to 1:30pm
Lunch $11.00 per person

Location

### *Guests are welcome*

Does your Estate Plan prepare your family for life without you?
Or
Does it merely transfer assets?

The Kelly Group at Smith Barney Invites You to

## "Family Estate Planning"

Guest Speaker
**Sandra Brown Sherman, Esq.**
Riker, Danzig, Scherer, Hyland & Perretti LLP

Thursday, March 23rd, 2006
6:30 - 9:00PM

Smith Barney Conference Room
400 Campus Drive
Florham Park, NJ 07932

Dinner will be served

You are invited to bring a guest
but seating is limited for this special event.

RSVP to:

# Post Event Review Form

# POST EVENT REVIEW FORM

Event: _____

Topic: _____

#RSVP: _____

Date: _____

Speaker: _____

#Attendees: _____

| Item | Rating 1-5 | Positive Comments | Negative Comments |
|---|---|---|---|
| **THE VENUE** | | | |
| • Environment | | | |
| • Space | | | |
| • Service/Staff | | | |
| • Food | | | |
| | | | |
| **PRESENTER** | | | |
| • Speaking skills | | | |
| • Focus on 3 key points | | | |
| • Supported Objectives | | | |

| Item | Rating 1-5 | Positive Comments | Negative Comments |
|---|---|---|---|
| **ENGAGING THE AUDIENCE** | | | |
| • Reception and introductions | | | |
| • High energy | | | |
| • Opening activity | | | |
| • Closing skills | | | |
| • Evaluation | | | |
| • Commitment | | | |
| • Created sense of urgency | | | |
| | | | |
| **OBJECTIVES** | | | |
| • RSVPs | | | |
| • Actual Attendees | | | |
| • Referrals and Introductions | | | |
| • Prospects vs. Clients | | | |
| • Final Commitment | | | |

| Item | Rating 1-5 | Positive Comments | Negative Comments |
|---|---|---|---|
| **FOLLOW UP** | | | |
| • Reached all participants | | | |
| • Engaged in conversation | | | |
| • Profiled prospect | | | |
| • Gained additional commitment | | | |
| • Generated new referral | | | |
| • Tracked results and information | | | |
| | | | |
| **What will I do differently with my next event based on the outcome of this event:** | | | |
| | | | |

# Sample Scripts

# QUALIFYING SCRIPTS

## Scenario #1:

**Adam:** "Hi Mr../Mrs../Ms. Doe. My name is Adam Sze and I am calling from the Kelly Group here at Smith Barney. We are very excited about our upcoming event and were hoping that we could reserve a place for both you and a guest. We sent you an invitation, does (date) at (time) work for you?

(If at that point they act as if this is the first they heard about the event then you can tell them you sent them an invitation and apologize for the delay then)

Then go into

**Prospect:** "Yes I did"

**Adam:** This Estate Planning seminar is an exclusive event for our clients that have at least $1 million of investable assets. We wanted to be sure you were included in this event.

**Prospect:** "Yes, that sounds interesting; may I ask what would be covered?"

**Adam:** "Sure, the event will be hosted by the Kelly Group one of Barron's Research Magazine "Top 100 Financial Advisors". The guest speaker will be Sandy Sherman a well-recognized estate attorney located right here in (city). What we have found is that most individuals feel that they have addressed all of their estate planning needs with their trust when in fact most of the families we have worked with have actually accomplished very little. In this event we will be discussing the most common pitfalls of most estate plans to make sure you have done what it takes to protect your family and your wealth.

Does (day and time) work for you?

**Prospect:** "Yes it does"

**Adam:** "Great, will your wife/husband be joining you? Great and why don't I pencil in that you will be bringing a guest? That way you can call me with a name later.

**Prospect:** "Yes/No/No Sure"

**Adam:** "In either case, dinner will be served and the seminar should be an educational and fun time. Hope to see you there. Thank you!"

**Scenario #2:**

**Adam:** "Hi Mr../Mrs../Ms. Doe. My name is Adam Sze and I am calling from the Kelly Group here at Smith Barney. The reason for my call today to see whether or not you have received the Estate Planning seminar initiation that we mailed to you."

**Prospect:** " Yes I did/I think I did I'm not sure"

**Adam:** "Great, the Estate Planning seminar we are having is an exclusive event for individuals with at least $1 million of investable assets. I was calling to see whether or not you would be interested in attending?"

**Prospect:** "Ha-ha, no I don't have that kind of money to invest!"

**Adam:** "Well in either case, we will be having many more educational seminars in the future. Tell me what are your greatest concerns regarding your investment portfolio?

**(NOW IS THE TIME TO START PROFILING)**

May we contact you again in the future to see if you would like to attend?

**Prospect:** "Yes/No"

## Scenario #3:

**Adam:** "Hi Mr../Mrs../Ms. Doe. My name is Adam Sze and I am calling from the Kelly Group here at Smith Barney. The reason for my call today is to see whether or not you have received the Estate Planning seminar invitation that we mailed to you."

**Prospect:** "No I did not"

**Adam:** "Well then let me tell you about this seminar we are hosting. The Estate Planning seminar we are having is an exclusive event for individuals with at least $1 million of investable assets. I was calling to see whether or not you would be interested in attending?"

**Prospect:** "Yes, that sounds interesting; may I ask what would be covered?"

**Adam:** "Sure, the event will be hosted by the Kelly Group one of Barron's Research Magazine "Top 100 Financial Advisors". The guest speaker will be Sandy Sherman, a well-recognized estate attorney from the firm Riker Dazing. Ms. Sherman will discuss the benefits of Estate Planning for High Net Worth individuals. May I add your name to our attendees list?"

**Prospect:** "Yes you may"

**Adam:** "Great, and will you be bringing a guest?"

**Prospect:** "Yes/No/No Sure"

**Adam:** "In either case, dinner will be served and the seminar should be an educational and fun time. Hope to see you there. Thank you!"

## FOLLOW UP:

Mr./Mrs. _____, this is Matthew Carroccio with Smith Barney, we recently invited you to an event that you were unable to attend. The response was so positive we are hosting the event again. As a quick reminder, this lunch is focused on The Changing Market Environment and our goal is for you to understand:

- How HNW individuals are using Hedge Funds and other alternative investments
- The importance of financial planning and
- Risk Management strategies you can use to reduce the volatility in your portfolio.

We have another lunch on April 20 at 12:00 Noon at Morton's on Connecticut Avenue and I wanted to see if this one might work with your schedule.

## NO:

Okay. Mr./Mrs. _____, we have been trying to get you to one of these lunches for a few months and obviously, our schedules are not working together. We believe that the information we discuss in these lunches is timely and is critical to the success of our clients meeting their financial goals. Since we have not been able to get you to one of our lunches, we would like to set up a 30-minute meeting to share this information with you. Normally, we like to meet in the morning and discuss this information over coffee. Are you free any morning in the next few weeks?

## NO:

Mr./Mrs. _____, we are both professionals and obviously very busy. I do not want to waste either of our time with continued calls. It is important to me that you let me know right now if you are interested in me continuing to contact you. I can add you to our email list and continue trying you for future lunches.

## STOP CALLING:

Okay, Mr./Mrs. _____, I wish you the best of luck with your financial planning and investments. My team believes we are in a changing market environment and risk management is extremely important. I hope that you have a plan in place with your current advisor to manage the risk in both your taxable investments and your 401(k). Would you be interested in receiving our periodic updates on the risk/reward potential of the markets?

## WAS NOT ABLE TO ATTEND:

Mr/Ms._____, this is Matthew Carroccio with Smith Barney. I am sorry you missed our lunch yesterday. The feedback was tremendous. As a result, we will be hosting this event again next month. As I mentioned to you in previous conversations, we host events on a monthly basis exclusively for partners in law firms. Our next lunch is on May 18 at 12:00 Noon at Morton's. I hope you are able to attend or we can get together and go over the presentation one morning over coffee. Please call me at ------ and let me know how you would like to proceed.

*Make them feel like they missed something. MAKE THEM JEALOUS…instill regret and remorse, and then give them hope. Talk to them like a friend: you should have gone. However, there is hope: I am doing this again, can I reserve you a place. The more I create an air of not needing them the better.*

# Sample Presentations

# INTRO AND CLOSING:

## Introduction

We would like to get started. First, thank you for taking the time from your busy careers to join us. We know you time is important and we promise to make the most of the next 45 minutes for you.

My name is Matthew Carroccio and this is my partner Tripp Shreves. Our team consists of two other partners and two assistants. Our business is focused on providing professionals and their families with financial planning and investment management advice. We understand that finances can be an issue of stress. For this reason, our goal is to bring consistency, balance and vision to our clients' financial lives.

One of the greatest challenges we face as Financial Consultants is that everyone is out to beat the market and because of this, most people end up losing more than the market on its way down. Most individual investors and many institutions do not have a strategic plan for market volatility. Here is an interesting statistic:

In 2002, the S&P 500 was down 22%. The average mutual fund investor actually lost more than 22%. However, high net worth investors on average lost only 3% of their money and Ultra HNW investors, those with more than 30MM in investable assets, averaged gains of 2.1% in 2002.

How many of you would like to beat the market?

From 1998 to present, the S&P 500 has been flat, if that continues for another 5 to 10 years, will you be able to meet you financial goals?

Last week we sent all of you some homework. That homework consisted of a four-page article that discusses the importance of investing to meet your necessary returns rather than investing to "beat the market". We also asked you to think about three questions:

1. Have you clearly defined your financial goals?
2. What rate of return do you need from your investments to meet those goals?
3. What risk management strategies do you have in place to help prevent serious loss while trying to meet those goals?

We answer all those questions for our clients to bring consistency, balance and vision to their financial lives.

Our goal today is not to scare you. Our goal is to educate you on the importance of having goals and managing your investments to meet that goal. Otherwise, you are just trying to beat an arbitrary index that has no relation to you or your future financial needs.

Tripp, why do not you share some financial market history and then discuss how many institutions and High Net Worth Families are investing to protect themselves and to ensure they meet their goals.

## Conclusion

Thanks, Tripp. Our group takes the philosophy of Yale and other institutions and we apply it to our clients. We look at each of our relationships as divided into three segments: Financial Planning, Risk Management and Wealth Management.

In Financial Planning, we look at where our clients are and where they want to be. We figure out how much they plan to add to their investments for the remainder of their career and then figure out what rate of return they need from their investments to achieve their goals. Once we know what rate of return they need, we develop a target asset allocation that we believe provides the best chance for you to meet your goals while taking on the least amount of risk.

Risk Management is looking at the risk reward potential of each asset class and increasing and decreasing exposure to each asset class accordingly.

Our Wealth Management platform is where we focus on the other aspects of our clients' financial lives such as insurance, lending, cash management and estate planning. These three segments of our business allow us to bring consistency, balance and vision to our clients' financial lives and help our clients reduce stress in their everyday lives.

If you think this makes sense and has the potential to add value, the next step is for us to sit down with you and review your financial situation to determine if this is a strategy that makes sense going forward. Money is money, but each of you are unique and our program is unique. Our investment philosophy is not for everyone, but the only way for us to know if it works for you is to sit down and take the next step of reviewing your financial situation.

For those who see the value in what we do and would like to take the next step with us, please check the box on this evaluation form (hold up) that you would like a personal portfolio review. For those of you who do not feel this is appropriate, thank you for coming and we hope you learned something that will be helpful to you in your future. If there are any other areas that you would like information on, please check off the box on this form. If you know of anyone who you think may be interested in attending one of these lunches in the future, there is an area for you to indicate that on the sheet. We also have a box for you to check if you would like to be added to our periodic market commentary email or our monthly wealth planning series email.

At this time, I will pass out these evaluation forms and we would like to answer any questions you may have. Thanks again for coming.

# About the Author

**Adri Miller-Heckman** is a senior executive financial services expert with extensive nationwide training experience in business development. Her 22-year tenure with the industry and 13 years with Smith Barney/ Citigroup includes positions as Sales Assistant, Branch Administrator, Financial Consultant, National Training Officer and Director of National Sales for Women and Co. a division of Citigroup. In addition to her training of over 2000 Financial Advisors Adri headed up the Smith Barney Multi-cultural Symposium, developed, and led many women's workshops addressing the issues unique to the female advisor.

In her current role as consultant and Coach to the Financial Advisor Adri provides one-on-one monthly coaching, group training programs as well as developmental workshops and motivational presentations. Adri has been a keynote speaker for a number of conferences that include, Smith Barney, Citigroup, Merrill Lynch in addition to independent firms such as Montauk Financial and WRP Investments. Adri is also an approved Financial Advisor Coach at Smith Barney, Merrill Lynch, Deutsche Bank, UBS, and Bank of America.

Adri specializes in helping the Advisor create strategic marketing plan that dramatically increases referrals, enhances client relationships, while freeing up more time to prospect and grow the business.

Adri developed and copyrighted The Total Wealth Advisor Program designed to create a simple proactive process to address total wealth management. This simple program has proven to be highly successful for both the Advisor as well as the client. This program doubles as a client service model as well as prospecting strategy.

In addition to writing this book, Adri Miller-Heckman provides one-on-one coaching as well as group teleconference programs designed to help advisors like you accelerate the development and success of their seminar programs. For more information visit:

www.AdriMillerConsulting.com

or email Adri directly at:

Adri@AdriMillerConsulting.com